201

A BALKAN EXCHANGE

A BALKAN EXCHANGE

Eight Poets from Bulgaria & Britain

Edited and introduced by
W. N. Herbert

PUBLICATIONS

new
writing
north

in association with
new writing north
2007

Published by Arc Publications
Nanholme Mill, Shaw Wood Road
Todmorden, Lancs OL14 6DA, UK

Design by Tony Ward
Printed by Biddles Ltd.
King's Lynn, Norfolk, UK

ISBN-13: 978 1904614 40 1

The publishers are grateful to the authors and translators and, in
the case of previously published works, to their publishers for
allowing their poems to be included in this anthology. Andy
Croft's poems have previously been published in *The London
Magazine, PN Review* and Claire Malcolm (ed.) *Magnetic North*.
Linda France's 'Stamps of Bulgaria' appeared in *Literatura
vestnik*, translated by Nadya Radulova.
  The authors acknowledge the support of the School of Eng-
lish at Newcastle University.
  Thanks are also due to the Northern Rock Foundation for
its support of the 'Balkan Exchange' project at its inception.

northern rock
foundation

The cover photograph was taken by Linda France in 2005
and is of a doorway in Ekzarh Jossif Street, Sofia, Bulgaria.

The publishers acknowledge financial assistance
from New Writing North and from Arts Council England, Yorkshire

LOTTERY FUNDED

**Arc Publications Translations series
Translation Editor: Jean Boase-Beier**

CONTENTS

VBV
Introduced by W. N. Herbert / 119

W. N. HERBERT

In the autumn of 2004, myself, British-Jordanian novelist Fadia Faqir, and fellow poet Mark Robinson, were invited by the British Council to work with six writers and two musicians on a series of performances around Sofia. This trip was set up and co-ordinated by Leah Davcheva, who was to become our tireless supporter, co-instigator of this book, and dear friend.

I had first visited Bulgaria as an adolescent on a day trip to the ancient seaport of Varna, an excursion from a Romanian package holiday. Bulgaria seemed very alien compared to the generic tourist beaches we were bussed away from: filled with the giant empty heroics of Communist statuary, it was at once poorer, forbidding and more intriguing, its Roman remains hinting at whole swathes of unknown history. When I returned thirty years later, I arrived in a different country in more than one sense.

My awareness of its complicated history had deepened: between the two poles of Rome and Moscow I was now able to string the successive resurgences and tragic collapses of the Byzantines and the early Orthodox kingdoms, the struggles with the Tatars and the Turks, the pivotal role of communist partisans in the Second World War, and that whole effort to maintain the identity of a small country continually being swamped then abandoned by machinating empires. But of its people and its poetry I knew almost nothing.

Sofia felt like a city subtly dislocated by its history: positioned in the would-be middle of a greater Bulgaria that had never materialised, its Soviet-style blocks of flats and wannabe European boulevards vied with more recently-arrived advertising hoardings and showy glass-fronted businesses. Façades were shabby, the statuary looked tired, and the grand buildings – Nevski Cathedral, the university with its earthquake-proof foyer, the Opera House that couldn't afford costumes – all seemed slightly too big for their settings.

As we drove from the airport I found myself immediately, instinctively, translating the Cyrillic of slogans, adverts and road signs in an attempt to make something familiar. Then I saw a black-clad art student turning her back on the very imposing Levski football stadium to draw what appeared to be a giant submachine-gun as it rose over some shopping booths and straggly autumn trees. This turned out to be a typical Eastern bloc war memorial in the city's central park, but the image came back to me as I met and began to work with Sofia's writers and realised they too were re-imagining their country in the wake of momentous change. We had all arrived in a shared moment of afterwards.

That first trip was a blast of new faces and new experiences – Plamen Doynov's wry greeting to the black marketeers at Sitnyakovo

Market before we began barking through megaphones; a strange synth-driven ambient performance in the cavernous foyer of the university; Toma Markov doing a rap in the high security wing of Sofia Prison that had all the prisoners stomping and clapping to the beat; the beer-fuelled final gig at a night club where the band, Bluba Lu, decided to wig out and improvise their backings to our carefully-prepared work. But throughout it I kept trying to assemble a collage of all the fragments of lines that we could get our fellow writers to translate. I remember being struck by a line from one poet who performed under the name 'VBV': 'I love you, my girl, my habit and border.'

I did a reading in a bookshop with two poets, Georgi Gospodinov and Nadya Radulova, an established and a rising star in the literary hierarchy, and the three of us were determined we had to do some translations of each other's work. We ended the event by reading out stanzas in each other's languages – their Scots was much better than my Bulgarian. Mark, Fadia and I all agreed the quality of the work we were catching in tiny glimpses was exceptional, and that a translation project seemed a natural next step. Georgi and Nadya were keen to publish translations of our work into Bulgarian. But the economics made such a project seem unlikely.

What we were all agreed on was that the link had to continue, and sure enough, the following spring I headed back to Sofia, this time travelling with Andy Croft, to deliver a course on teaching creative writing techniques. We had noticed that the standard tools of the creative exercise and discursive workshop we were so used to in Britain simply didn't exist in Bulgaria, and Leah Davcheva, again co-ordinating our visit, saw an opportunity to share skills. Andy and I worked with twelve writers, including Georgi, Nadya and (VBV's 'real' name) Vassil Vidinsky. Among the new faces this time was the laconic, witty Kristin Dimitrova. After long days working together, we would spent the evenings discussing politics and poetry in both our countries, and, of course, still scheming as to how we could put together a translation project.

At the end of this week, Leah took Andy and I on a trip to Gara Thompson, the small railway station in the mountains around Sofia named after Frank Thompson, the brother of the historian E.P. Thompson, who had fought and died with the partisans during the Second World War. As we stood in the shambles of an almost derelict mining town to read his plaque, then drove around the steep cliff-faces and descending curtains of limestone, where generations of rebels had ambushed the Turks, and finally climbed a small hill outside the village of Litakovo to the common grave where Thompson was buried after being shot by the fascists, I could see that Andy, like

myself, was bonding with this stubborn, distinctive, lovely place.

Mark Robinson, meanwhile, had travelled separately to the old university town of Plovdiv for a conference involving writers and arts administrators from across the Balkans, and came back equally determined that some further contact had to be made. At this point we began talking to Claire Malcolm, Director of the North East's writers' agency, New Writing North, and she and Leah put together a project to bring four writers over to Newcastle for a week to embark on a book of translations.

At the back of both Mark's head and mine was the method used by the old European Translation Network, which we had taken part in at the Tyrone Guthrie Centre at Annaghmakerrig in Ireland. The then Director of Poetry Ireland, Theo Dorgan, had assembled a team of poets to translate poets from all over Europe. Visiting poets would arrive in pairs, accompanied by translators and literals, and two complete books would be produced over a week of intensive workshops. Could we attempt something similar?

Reluctantly we realised that prose would be too complicated to include, and settled for a pairing of four British and four Bulgarian poets – Georgi, Nadya, Vassil and Kristin were all able to come and, between them, had good to brilliant English. Leah suggested Boris Deliradev both to accompany them and do the literals, and we suggested Linda France as the fourth British writer. There was just one fly in the chilled yoghurt soup: I didn't want just to do a book of translations.

It seemed to me that this project was as much about an encounter between people and places as it was about an encounter with texts. It was about the collisions and interactions of cultures, not just the friendships formed but the shifts in our historical imaginations. I thought that if this was to be a properly engaged and engaging aesthetic document it had to find a way of encapsulating all these levels of experience.

So I suggested that the translations and the culture should be approached through the creative sensibilities of the translators – and that this should be a reciprocal arrangement. So the British poets should include their own poems about visiting Bulgaria – not as touristic notes, but as maps of the type of engagement found in the translations, as intros, filters and shadows. And, equally, there should not be one book, but two: one in English, and another attempting the same task in Bulgarian.

One consequence of this was that the Bulgarian poets weren't simply taking part in a translation project, they were beginning a relationship with this country, particularly our home territories of Hexham,

Newcastle and Middlesbrough: the North East. Another consequence was that Linda, having met and worked with Georgi, Nadya, Kristin and Vassil, then had to visit them in Sofia, an experience she writes about elsewhere in this book.

Our work method for the translations was simple. We booked two adjacent rooms in Newcastle University's School of English. Linda and I paired up, as did Mark and Andy. Since Nadya and Kristin had the better English, they paired up with Georgi and Vassil respectively. Then we worked, poem by poem, through a body of work Boris had prepared in roughs. We swopped translatees (or they swopped translators) every day or so, with Boris moving between the groups as needed. Then, when we had rough first drafts, we came together and worked as a single unit to produce more polished drafts that were as idiomatic as each poet or each poem demanded. Then, finally, work was posted on a blog for comments, adjustments, and, crucially, so that it could just mature. The result is the book you hold.

W . N. Herbert

A BALKAN EXCHANGE

KRISTIN DIMITROVA
Introduced by Andy Croft

KRISTIN DIMITROVA may be described as a Balkan minimalist, a fabulist whose work combines the fabulous and the prosaic. She writes with a deceptively simple, playful, light touch, teasing the reader with faux-folk-wisdom and her unexpected, often deliberately bathetic endings. Oblique, subtle and witty, her poems creep up on her subjects from behind, demonstrating that looking at something sideways is not the same as avoiding the issue.

The first time I met Kristin I thought I had upset her. We were talking about poetry and tradition in a bar in Sofia. She seemed to be disagreeing profoundly with everything I said. Each attempt at clarification produced another violent shake of her head. It was only later I remembered that in Bulgaria a nod of the head means No and a shake of the head means Yes. The incident captures an important quality of Dimitrova's poetry – apparently disagreeing with the world, while vigorously assenting to be a part of it.

It is hard to overstate the importance of Kristin's writing in contemporary Bulgaria. Described by one critic as 'one of the most imitated female poets in Bulgarian literature', her poetry has been widely praised for helping to introduce 'erudition and witty invention, poetic experience and intellectual self-reflection' into the tradition of women's writing in Bulgaria.

Kristin's literary awards include five national 'poetry of the year' awards, one for poetry performance in Stockholm, two awards for her short stories and one for her pioneering translations of John Donne's poetry into Bulgarian. It is not difficult to see why she is attracted to a poet who successfully combined the witty and the religious, the playful and the dramatic, the sexual and the tragic all at the same time. Like Donne's poetry, her work demonstrates that poetry does not have to be moralizing in order to be great.

She has also published a best-selling collection of short stories, *Life and Death under the Crooked Pear Trees* (in Bulgarian the title means 'nowhere; not at a place to be proud of'), combining the real and the fantastic, the logical and the unexpected. She is currently adapting one of the stories into a screen play.

Kristin Dimitrova is recognized as being in 'the vanguard of a new movement... trying to give an answer to the essential questions of the downfall of Bulgaria', part of 'a literary renaissance that may finally realize the dream of our nineteenth-century authors: a uniquely Bulgarian cultural voice, the equal of any in the world.'

Andy Croft

ЛЮБОВНА ИСТОРИЯ

Те играеха помежду си –
той – с главата й,
тя – с краката му.
После той й върнал главата,
малко поизхабена,
а тя – не разбрах
какво направила с краката му,
дотук знам историята.

ВРЕМЕНАТА

Сега двамата се изкачваха по пътеката
и с тихи гласове обсъждаха съжителството
между съдбата, новините в 8
и собствените си защитни действия.

В далечината слънцето прокапваше през клоните,
но някак се чуждееше. Листата,
майчински загърнати от скреж,
брояха дните си.

Какво обичахме?
Кой как започна?

Той, прагматикът, днес се дави в музиката,
а тя, художничката, стана бримка
по пътя на коприната.

На просеката двама влъхви хапваха консерва,
събираха сезонна топлина и се оглеждаха за третия,
отбил се по-нагоре в храсталаците.

Променливо е времето. Пророците
останаха без работа.

LOVE STORY

They played games with each other –
he with her head,
she with his legs.
Then he gave back her head,
a little worn out,
and she – I'm not sure
what she did with his legs,
this is as much as I know.

TIMES

The two of them were walking up the path,
quietly discussing the menage
of fate, the 10 o'clock news
and their own defensive strategies...

In the distance the sun dripped through the branches,
refusing to communicate. The leaves,
tucked up in frost,
counted down their days.

Who loved what?
How did we get here?

He, once so practical, is now drowning in music,
she, the artist, is just a stitch
along the silk road.

In a clearing two magi ate out of a can,
making the most of the thin light, waiting for the third,
who had disappeared into the bushes.

Changeable times.The prophets
have lost their jobs.

СДАВАНЕ НА БАГАЖА

Този човек
беше невинен,
защото нямаше нищо общо
с живота, макар че
оттам се връщаше.
Дай си обратно зъбите –
каза една вълшебна ръка
и го прасна в устата.
Човекът се огледа
за последно, благодари
за припека, а на
излизане извика:
„И вше пак, беше шкапано!"

ПОЧИВКА НА МОРЕ

Цвъртене на плажно масло.
Жегата ни е захлупила
като оловна уста –

не се пробива от крясъците,
играта на топка
не я разтваря.

Лежим в различни пози
и с това доказваме,
че все още нещо

зависи от нас.
В далечината тънка лодка
бяга към белия ръб на морето –

без въжета зад себе си, без колебания,
без спасители на гърба,
без задух...

– Без коз.

PASSING ON

This man
was innocent,
he had nothing to do
with life, although
that's where he was coming from.
'Give back your teeth'
a magic hand said
and smacked him in the mouth.
The man looked round
one last time, gave thanks
for the sunshine, and
as he left cried out,
'It washn't worsh the hasshle.'

SEASIDE HOLIDAY

The sizzling of sunscreen.
The heat has closed over us
like a mouth made of lead –

shouting won't break it,
beach games
won't lift it.

We lie in various positions
trying to prove
that we still

make some choices.
In the distance a tiny boat
is hurrying towards the white edge of the sea –

no moorings, no doubts,
no life guards,
no suffocation...

'No trumps...'

ВЕЧЕРИНКА В ПАНСИОНА НА САКАТИТЕ

Сред недопълнени фигури
певецът пееше една
широка песен и аз го предупредих,
че реката е прекалено близо зад него, а той
ме заведе до ръба и ме бутна.
Вкопчена в него, аз го завляках надолу
и докато летяхме към камъните
го попитах защо го направи. Имах
време да чуя и отговора:
„За да ти покажа,
че не е шега.”

ПОЕТЪТ И ОТВОРЪТ ПО СРЕДАТА МУ
На Марк Странд

Гадеше му се от смъртта – тя го караше
да живее прекалено ясно, прекалено
напрегнато. Понякога му се струваше,
че го наблюдава и тогава
ставаше суетен, говореше
енигматични глупости по интервютата,
тайно изпъваше гръб и разкопчаваше горното копче на ризата.
После рисуваше острови, за да му мине.
Освен това тя беше небрежна – забравяше
свои бележки в чекмеджето с писмата му,
дописваше му страниците.
В задния план на мечтите си
често зърваше профила й – разбира се,
съвсем за кратко, пък и никога не е сигурно
какво си видял – тънка фигура
в топлата плитка вода на лагуна,
сред стеблата на палмите
(и той, като другите, садеше палми
в мечтите си).

Сякаш му махаше.
Може би се усмихваше.
Вероятно на себе си.
        (Само иска да ме разстрои.)

PARTY AT THE HOME FOR THE DISABLED

Among the incomplete figures
the singer crooned
a vast song. I warned him
that the river was right behind, but he
led me to the edge and pushed.
Clutching him I pulled us down.
As we fell towards the rocks,
I asked why he'd done it. There was still
time for me to hear his reply:
'Just to show you
nothing's a joke.'

THE POET WITH THE HOLE IN HIS MIDDLE
For Mark Strand

Death made him sick. She pushed him
to live too clearly, too
intensely. Sometimes he felt
she was watching him and so
he would preen, speak
enigmatic gibberish in interviews,
secretly puff out his chest and undo the top button of his shirt.
Then he would paint islands to let go.

At the same time she was negligent, forgot
she'd left notes in his desk drawer,
completed his drafts.
In the background to his daydreams
he would often catch her profile – only for a second
of course, and you can never be sure
what you've seen – through the palm trees
in the warm shallows of a lagoon,
a thin figure
(like most people, he planted palm trees
in his dreams).

Perhaps she was waving at him.
Maybe she was smiling.
Possibly to herself.
        (She just wants to upset me.)

В ярост хвърляше остри думи към нея и
някои улучваха хартията, а други
се чупеха в огледалото.

А голямата тайна, празният отвор в гърдите му,
се разширяваше. Насаме, с разкопчана риза,
той го гледаше, опипваше боязливо ръбовете му,
надничаше в непознатия хоризонт отвътре и
напрягаше разум как да го прегради.
Всяка напречна мисъл отлиташе, всмукана
от смаляващата я тъмнина.

Тази вечер отворът
си беше на мястото. Смъртта
се подаде през него:
– Здрасти. Едно кафе?

(Значи все пак се върна.)

– Да, моля те,
черно.

ПРИЯТЕЛЮ,

извит на върбова клонка,
кой ти отне името?
Защо се вее тази квитанция за неплатен ток
от устата ти?
Гледам те, тук, висиш от прозореца,
пребоядисан от изгрева,
недообелен от залеза,
все в същия ден.
Срамота е.
Приятелю,
нанизан на тел през сърцето,
кой ти държи телта?
Други приятели, но това е
най-малкото.

In a fury he would hurl sharp words at her –
some would blot his papers, others
would shatter in his mirror.

His big secret, the empty hole in his chest,
dilated. Alone, shirt unbuttoned,
he would examine it, tentatively tracing the edges,
squint at the unlikely horizon inside,
baffled by how to plug it.
Every lateral solution was sucked away, shrinking
into darkness.

This evening the hole
was in place. Death
poked her head through it.
'Hi. Want to go for a coffee?'

(So she's back again.)

'Yes, let's.
I take mine black.'

MY FRIEND,

bent like a willow tree branch,
who took away your name?
Why is that unpaid electricity bill
dangling from your mouth?
I see you hanging out of your window,
freshly painted by sunrise,
untouched by the sunset,
always stuck in the same day.
It's a shame.
My friend,
strung on a wire through your heart,
who is holding the wire?
Other friends of mine,
but that is the least of my worries.

ИЗКУСТВОТО НА „СЛАВЕЙКОВ"

Вятърът роши
рехавите листа на стихосбирките,
смушкани в ъгъла на подвижния щанд.
Някои са така олисяли, че под корицата виждаш
как е ресано: десният кичур наляво,
               левият кичур надясно.
Валцованите им лобове са се надигнали,
за да призоват за сетен път към внимание
иззад катедрата в празната зала. По микрофона
се чува въздишка,
неловко засмиване,
и някакк повтарящо се изречение, което
не свършва от уста на уста, пробива
тила и излиза през гърлото,
и така е пришило един за друг авторите:

„Животът беше кратък като ден
и обещаваше, че има смисъл".

Младите рошави книжки се трупат отгоре им,
викат по-силно, по-добре знаят какво, но като цяло
са недохранени като футболна агитка от краен квартал,
след загубата на фаворита.

„Ний сме по-краси-ви и сме по-добри!"

Виковете се удрят в сателитните чинии и
отскачат, защото тече следващият репортаж.
Животът е все така важен. Въпросът е

кой ще го каже.

КАРТИЧКА ДО ЗЕЛЕНИТЕ БРАТЯ

Звездни поздрави!
Изпращаме
звездни поздрави!
Ние тук сме добре
и редовно
си вземаме хапчетата.

ART ON SLAVEIKOV SQUARE

The wind riffles through
the thin pages of poetry
crowded in the corner of the bookstall.
Some of them are losing their hair – you can see it
through the covers: hair from the right is combed to the left,
                    hair from the left is combed to the right.
They have raised their round heads
to demand attention one last time, from behind
the lectern in the empty auditorium. A sigh
can be heard in the microphone,
an awkward laugh,
and a line that gets repeated by everyone
goes from mouth to mouth, straight through
the back of the head, and comes out at the throat,
stitching the poets together:

'Life proved so short a day
and once promised so much meaning.'

The young books, dishevelled, piled on top of the old ones,
shout louder, know just what to say, but are
underfed as football fans from a sink estate
after losing to the champions.

'Wearethegreatestteam
theworldhaseverseen!'

The cries hit the satellite dishes
and bounce back – the next news bulletin is on.
Life is as important as it ever was. The question is
who breaks the news.

POSTCARD TO OUR BROTHERS, THE LITTLE GREEN MEN

Celestial greetings!
Accept our
celestial greetings!
We are all fine
down here, we keep
taking our pills.

ПРИЕМЕН ИЗПИТ

Всички слушаха,
разкроени в дълбоки редици
като китайската теракотена армия.
Бяха втренчили голите си глави –
обли, като яйца на птеродактили,
и очакваха някакъв жест, който
най-сетне
окончателно
ще дискредитира говорещия.
        – Та… исках да кажа…
Те слушаха.
        – , че свободата не се появява с нас,
        както например ръце и два крака,
        ако имаш късмет, от самото
        начало…
Някои глави се сближиха озадачено
по двойки, или може би
на говорещия така му се стори.
        – …Ммм, в смисъл, че
        не ни е присъща,
        не ни се полага от самосебе си…
        (Не говоря ли адски банални неща?)
Те се облегнаха възмутено назад
и наостриха вежди.
        – А после родителите,
        училището, службата, обществото
        някакси… те желаят,
        без обаче да те харесват.
        Пък аз искам да ме харесват.
– Аааа – премина през залата почти осезателно.
        (Значи не ми се е сторило!)
        – … и тогава аз,
        дето цял живот съм искал
        да кандидатствам за тук
и да стана един от вас, разбирам, …
Част от валчестите глави се спогледаха.
Чу се проскърцване на изместен камък.
        – че винаги
        съм ви принадлежал
        и свободата е само
        ако намразиш наградите си,
        хванеш свързващите въжета
        и режеш! режеш! режеш!…
Една от глинените глави
се търкулна.

EXAMINATION

They were all listening,
drawn up in columns
like a Chinese terracotta army.
They stared, their bald heads
round as pterodactyls' eggs,
waiting for a gesture
that would finally
and conclusively
discredit the candidate.
    'Er... what I was about to say...'
They listened.
    '... is that freedom is not something we are born with,
    the way we are born with two hands and two legs,
    if we are lucky, that is...'
Some of the heads bent towards each other, puzzled
or so the speaker suspected.
    '... E-er, I mean that
    freedom is not inherent in us,
    it is not a given...'
    (Wasn't that ridiculously trite?)
They sat back indignantly
and sharpened their eyebrows.
    'and then parents,
    teachers, colleagues, society,
    they all somehow... want you
    but they don't like you.
    And I want to be liked...'
'Aah' – the room almost stirred.
    (So I wasn't imagining!)
    '... and then I,
    who have wanted
    to come here all my life
    and be one of you, I understand...'
Some of the boulder heads looked at each other.
A shifting rock groaned.
    'I have always
    belonged to you,
    and that freedom comes
    when you reject the prizes,
    grab the ropes
    and start cutting! cutting! cutting!...'
A clay head
rolled down.

ПО-СКОРО УЮТНА

По-скоро уютна
е липсата на слънце
в тази бавна сутрин –

държа се с две ръце
за кафето си, а
ти, живакът в аматьорската

ми алхимия, някак хрисимо
улучваш устата си
с хляб и сирене,

с поглед, подпрян на вестника.
Иззад кръглото стъкло
прозрачните очи на костенурките

виждат как двамата
изчезваме в неподвижността си
и от време на време

се появява ръка, протегната
към захарта, или
уста, обърната надолу

в усмивка.

СПОМЕНИ ОТ СТУДЕНАТА ВОЙНА

Казваха ни,
че има два враждуващи свята,
но имаше само един.

Ние бяхме
от другия.

IT'S ALMOST COSY

It's almost cosy,
the lack of sun
on this slow morning

I hold on with both hands
to my coffee cup while you –
the mercury in my homespun

alchemy – somehow manage
to put cheese and bread
in your mouth quietly,

gaze fixed on the newspaper.
From inside their bowl
the turtles' transparent eyes

follow how we both
vanish into stillness
and how from time to time

a hand appears
reaching for the sugarbowl,
or a mouth curves downwards

into a smile.

COLD WAR MEMORIES

We were told
there were two worlds at war
when there was really only one.

We were
the other.

ПИШЕЩИЯТ ЧОВЕК

Сигурна съм, че
не смяташе себе си
за малък.
Поколеба се дали
да пресече и в последния момент
хвана автобуса.
Не съм го видяла как
е успял да се изкатери
по стъпалата.
– Как се казваш ти? А?
Как се казваш? – питаха
грижовните лелки, надушили
нещо нередно.

Той не отговори.

По цялото му лице бяха изписани
сложни фигури с химикалка –
ромб с точка в средата върху едната буза
се свързваше с отсрещната вежда,
задрасквайки всичко по пътя си.

– Майка му сега ще полудее
от ужас! Ами да! Ще полудее
от ужас – тюхкаха се грижовните
лелки.

Най-вероятно
той не можеше да говори,

но цяла сутрин бе писал писма
по лицето си и тези, които наистина
се интересуваха, можеха
да прочетат:

– Няма кой да полудее от ужас
за мене.

Автобусът отвори врати за нови хора и там някъде
той изчезна.

THE WRITER

I am sure
he didn't see himself
as a kid.
He hesitated before crossing
and then at the last moment
jumped on the bus.
I don't know how
he managed the steps.

'What's your name, pet?
What's your name?' asked
the fussy old biddies, sensing
that something was wrong.

He didn't reply.

His face was scrawled with
complicated shapes –
a line from one cheek to the opposite eyebrow
connected a lozenge with a dot,
striking through everything on its way.

'His mother will be worried sick!
Yes, she will! She will be
so worried,' the old women fretted.

It was quite possible
he could not talk yet,

but he had spent the morning writing letters
on his face, and those who
cared to could read:

'I have no-one to be worried sick
about me.'

The doors opened to let more people on
and that's where I lost him.

ТРИ КОРАБА

Три кораба пътуваха.
Единият пренасяше коприна.
А вторият се движеше към нищото.
Последният се връщаше назад
към свят от оцелели митове.

Помахахме си.

Три пъти сменям кораба и
все е същият.

ЕДНА ОДИСЕЯ В 2002

Някога тук нямаше пукнат магазин,
а сега толкова много се разпукаха.
Булевардът на грима и козметиката
пак е набръчкан, но с нова дентура.
Два потока народ напуска
срещуположни трамваи пред Халите
и смила някаква жена по средата.
За известно време в мелето едната й вежда
сочи към сергията за геврец,
а другата – към Сириус, ако можеше да се види
през облаците.
2001 вече мина
без Одисея,
без малка стъпка за човека,
        но голяма за човечеството,
        без Голямата стъпка.
Мечтите на 60-те отдавна са
        разредени и бутилирани
в лосион за пърхот с подсилено действие
и сме тъжни сега,
и сме радостни, защото
        си искаме лосиона.
Продавачката е напрегната.
        – Блуза с мрежест ръкав, да,
        имаме плетени.

THREE SHIPS

There were three ships.
One was carrying silk.
The second was sailing into nothingness.
The third was coming back
from a world of enduring myths.

We waved at each other.

Three times I jumped ship
and I'm still on the same one.

2002: AN ODYSSEY

There wasn't a single bloody shop here
and now they're popping up all over.
The main street for make-up and skincare
is still wrinkled, but it's got new teeth.
Two streams of people spill out
of trams converging on the Hali Market
and sweep a woman up between them.
For a moment in the scrum one of her eyebrows
points at the bagel kiosk,
the other at Sirius, if it could be seen
through the clouds.
2001 has passed
with no Odyssey,
no small step for man,
        no giant leap for mankind.
The dreams of the 60s have long ago
        been diluted and bottled
as extra-strength dandruff shampoo
and now we are sad,
and we are happy, because
        we want our shampoo.
The shop assistant is stressed out.
        'A top with fish-net sleeves? Yes,
        we have knitted ones.'

– Плетени? Абе вие, хора,
MTV не гледате ли?
питам аз, заровена в закачалките,
а мразя MTV,
ама как да не й го зачукаш.

'Knitted? Don't
you people watch MTV?'
I burrow among the clothes rails.
I don't even like MTV
but I can't resist the last word.

ANDY CROFT

WINE, ROSES AND POISONED UMBRELLAS

Red wine, red roses and Black Sea beaches, poisoned umbrellas and 'one-legged Bulgarian roofers' – it is safe to say that most people in Britain have only a very slight acquaintance with Bulgaria. It's a holiday resort, a sinister and alarming place and a fairy-tale Ruritanian kingdom. According to recent research by the British Council in Sofia, most British citizens think that Bulgaria (rather than 'Vulgaria') was the setting for the film *Chitty Chitty Bang Bang*.

There are probably even fewer literary associations for British readers. Orpheus is said to have been born in Thrace. The Cyrillic alphabet was invented in Bulgaria. The English poet Frank Thompson, who fought with the Bulgarian partisans in the Second World War, was executed near Sofia in 1944. During the Cold War the work of the Communist poet Nikola Vaptsarov was available in English translation. Eric Ambler's thriller *The Dark Frontier* and Malcolm Bradbury's comedy *Rates of Exchange* are set in the Balkan countries of 'Ixania' and 'Slaka', both generally thought to be based on Bulgaria. Julian Barnes's novel, *The Porcupine*, is a veiled fictional portrait of ex-premier Todor Zhivkov. Boris Akunin's international best-seller (also now a blockbusting film) *Turkish Gambit* is set in Bulgaria during the Russo-Turkish War of Liberation. Forest Books have recently published Bulgarian poets like Milev, Levchev and Davidkov. But that's about it. While Russian, Czech, Polish and even Romanian writers have long been part of our sense of a common European literature, Bulgarian writers have hitherto remained outside it.

For a thousand years Bulgaria was the border between Christian Europe, Orthodox Russia and Ottoman Islam; during the Cold War it was on the front-line between East and West; today it represents the vivid clash of the Traditional and the Modern. But in the globalised village life of the twenty-first century, Bulgaria is now our near neighbour. In 2004 Bulgaria joined NATO; an agreement allowing for the building of US military bases was signed in 2006. In January 2007 Bulgaria became a full member of the EU.

Bulgaria is changing rapidly. And so is its poetry. Of the young poets presented as 'the youthful and unbroken face of Bulgaria' in *Young Poets of a New Bulgaria* (Forest Books, 1990), two have since died, one has gone into exile in the USA, some are better known now as journalists or politicians (including the extreme right-wing Volen Siderov). If politics consumed the immediate post-Communist generation of Bulgarian poets, their successors keep an ironic distance from the political sphere. That's not to say that they do not address political issues, but that their approach is more oblique, less urgent, qualified by the disappointments of the last fifteen years. Where older poets wrote for a single reading public, or stood beneath the unifying banners of great political

causes, today's Bulgarian poets talk in more subdued tones in smaller groups defined by friendship and generation.

THERE WAS A SPIRIT IN EUROPE

'When I died at Marathon, I saw this only:
By my head the fennel was growing, slowly.'
Frank Thompson, 1941

'After the firing squad – the worms.'
Nikola Vaptsarov, 1942

Litakovo. The garlic breath of Spring
Begins to thaw the feet of these old hills,
Warm welcome for returning cranes who'll bring
The luck that resurrects what Winter kills.

The frozen fields below begin to stir
From heavy dreams of snow. The flowers keep
Their vigil for Persephone. The year
Turns over slowly, after months of sleep.

Cold-fingered Boreas, foundation-king
Of these cold hills, once wrestled with the sun
To prove that he was stronger than the Spring,
Half froze the world to stone, and almost won.

Two hours and several centuries ago
We left Sofia's beggared streets behind,
Through silent fields still scorched by months of snow,
Up hair-pin mountain roads. We crash and grind

Between the Iskar Gorge's narrow walls,
The thin-ribbed valley sides, the railway line,
Slow monasteries and urgent water-falls,
Steep, limestone-dazzle ridges furred with pine.

Prokopnik. Here, May 1944,
The Second Sofia (Partisan) Brigade
Passed into History, legend, silence, war.
The place they crossed the river's now decayed

Into a railway stop of weeds and rust
Beneath an iron mountain made of slag,
Where snow falls grey with coal-breath dirt and dust.
Prometheus upon his midnight crag.

This is a bleak and plundered place, a true
Memorial to the young man with a pipe
Depicted on the platform, after who
The station's named in carved Cyrillic type:

Frank Thompson, British Major, SOE,
A Wykhamist, a linguist, poet and Red,
A scion of the English bourgeoisie
Who found in Aeschylus the road that led

Him here to try to set the world ablaze,
To prove the new was stronger than the old
And almost won; heroic, Springtime days,
Defeated by the armies of the cold.

Across the other side they lost their way,
As we do too, through villages of cow
And breeze-block, where half-naked infants play
And Boreas's children pull the plough,

Where women still leave apples for the dead,
Inter red-pepper-phallused dolls to bring
The rain, and wear the martenitza thread
To bind the Easter rituals of Spring.

To Eleshnitsa (Easter Monday). Here
Where young men pitch-fork straw upon their backs,
They tortured Thompson. Roads that seem so clear
On maps turn out to be just snow-lined tracks

That disappear into the hills around
Litakovo, to which the Fascists brought
The captured partisans, this barrow mound
Among the trees they call the Turkish Fort.

Five common graves of cracked and lichened stone,
Is all that's left to show where they were shot,
A green memorial, wild and overgrown
For heroes whom the Winter world's forgot.

Their chiseled names now filigreed with moss,
The five-point star's an ivy-fingered hand
Reproaching the cold future with the loss
Of what we are ashamed to understand.

Though better known memorials than these
Have been knocked down by Winter's wolfish tread,
Obscurity's preserved, among these trees,
The short and simple annals of the dead

Who died for truths that no-one now believes,
Whose posthumous denunciations lie
Upon this woodland grave like fallen leaves –
First national hero, then a British spy,

Now Soviet agent. Winter's cold estate
Requires a hard forgetting. So the truth
They knew at Marathon, the Scaean Gate,
Becomes a frozen elegy for youth.

The beech's opening bud's a falling leaf,
Tomorrow is as cold as yesterday,
The seeds of Change have shrunk to the belief
That nothing lasts and all things must decay;

The North Wind blows the petals from the rose,
The Winter wolf destroys the Spring-born lamb,
The cow-slip meadow's crushed beneath the snows,
The child is sacrificed and not the ram;

The ploughed field disinters the buried god,
The sharpened sickle cuts the harvest wheat,
The prisoner has to face the firing-squad,
And victory's just a name we give defeat.

MARTENITSA

Long, long ago, there was a king
    Who put his foes to flight,
And the victory colours of the spring
    Were bannered red and white.

And the colour of blood is red,
    And white are the snows that fall,
And despite the blood that kings have shed
    The spring belongs to all.

And the victory march of the sun will thaw
    The blood that stains the snow
And hope will spring in the earth once more
    And the red roses grow.

KARTICHKA OT SOFIA

Just round the corner from the new hotel
That someone says was built by Russian mafia,
A kind of multi-alphabet dysgraphia
Now flourishes on tree-lined walls which spell
'Red Madness!', 'Lokomotib', 'HeHoHATO',
'bHC', 'Cockney Sparrers Oi! Oi! Oi!',
'CCCP', 'CSKA', 'Destroy!'
Town-planners and utopians since Plato
Have found their well-drawn plans a palimpsest
Through which the scrawl of Babel-tongued graffiti
Can still be read – part threat and part entreaty –
Return of the repressed, in lines addressed
To those who read the writing on the wall
From those who aren't supposed to write at all.

ROTUNDA

The woman lights another tapered prayer,
Whose weeping wax now gutters in the gloom,
A ritual task which only can illume
A world of superstition and despair.
Above us, in the bright empyrean blue,
The frieze of flaky prophets on the ceiling
Is laced with holes, as if the heavens were peeling
To let the pagan night beneath show through.

Behind each fading fresco lies the next,
Precise as tree-rings, measuring the ages
Of human hope and terror, like a text
Still legible beneath the parchment pages'
Faint palimpsest. As if such monkish art
Could ever warm this heartless world's cold heart.

THE BARON MUNCHAUSEN BAR, SOFIA
For Bill

'We drink, we sing with recklessness,
We snarl against the tyrant foe,
The taverns are too small for us,
"To the mountains we shall go." '
H. Botev

You follow the yellow-brick road through the snow,
Past the topless young girls on the highway,
Through Horrible Valley and Terrible Pass
Till at last you will come to a doorway.

It's tucked between Schweik's and Flanagan's Bar,
Down a side-street of uneven cobbles,
But once you're inside you know you're with friends
Who will help you forget all your troubles.

Inside it's so crowded and smoky and dark
That you can't tell one hand from the other;
Here a Yes means a No and a No means a Yes,
And the neighbouring sexes mean either.

You hang up your hang-ups just inside the door
In exchange for a small token gesture,
Sly Peter will offer to buy you a beer
And ask you to drink to the future.

And after a while you can see that it's full
Of artists in shades and black leather,
Like talking heads chained in the inferno-dark
They talk of new sins and old lovers.

Here the bar-maids are lovely as Catherine the Great,
And the beer tastes as cold as the Iskar;
On TV the football is never nil-nil,
And the Hristos are wrapping up Moskva.

And the peppers are red as CSKA shirts,
And the vegetable soup is near solid
With the flesh of the Chopski, that gentlest of tribes
Who taught us all how to make salad.

Here the regulars vote for a fairy-tale-king,
Who it's rumoured supports Barcelona,
He doesn't like children but comes in to drink
With the tough-looking boys in the corner.

Each night if you want you can drink the bar dry
As long as the Baron has credit,
Though the menu's as large as the Vitosha hills,
The bill is so small you can't read it.

If ever you leave here (and some never do)
You will find that the snow is still falling,
In Batenberg Square they've forgotten the date,
And the frozen tongued bells have stopped pealing;

And the skate-boarders spin round the partisan dead
In the gardens on Boulevard Levski,
And the tomb of Dimitrov's been swapped overnight
For an oversize bottle of whisky;

And the past is as clean as the streets under snow,
And everyone's tired and sleepy,
And the future's as bright as the man in the moon,
And freedom makes everyone happy;

And the statues outside are stiff with the cold,
And the girls by the road are still topless;
And the children of beggars are sleeping outside,
And the cold constellations are helpless.

The Baron untethers one half of his horse
Which he tied to an Orthodox steeple,
And wishes us all a merry goodnight
As he flies off to Constantinople.

Some say he's a con-man, some say he's for real,
Some say that the Baron's in earnest,
But don't take my word for it, go there yourself –
You'll never believe it all. Honest.

GEORGI GOSPODINOV
Introduced by Mark Robinson

GEORGI GOSPODINOV is very much part of both Balkan and European traditions. He plays a key role in Bulgarian literary and intellectual life, but also increasingly in the wider South-East Europe, where his work has been widely translated and he is a cult figure for the younger generation. His work combines a fascination with language, history, identity and love that is perfect for a region redefining itself after communism, war and the introduction of MTV.

Georgi's particular stature was made apparent to me in 2005, returning from Plovdiv to Sofia airport with some Bosnian poets. I had read his poem 'Gabriela's Dog' to an audience including all the nationalities mentioned – in halting Bulgarian and our then fresh English translation. The Bosnian poets were agog I'd been working with such a figure. His *Natural Novel* was, I was told, the defining book for the younger generation not just in Bulgaria but also the former Yugoslavia. It captured a peculiarly Balkan mix of alienation and connection.

I had not gathered this from the modest Gospodinov himself. It had, however, been clear from all our interactions with Bulgarian writers that he was the unspoken leader, the figure whose writing and demeanour set the tone. It was also clear to us that this was in opposition – or at the very least in a contrasting manner – to earlier generations. Born in 1968, Gospodinov has been important in investigating the legacy of socialism for him and younger writers, not least through his involvement in the 'I've lived socialism' memory project.

His poems are plain and enigmatic, layered with history and literary reference. They have a dry sense of humour and a pulse of romantic idealism beating beneath their sometimes calm skin. Language and literature themselves are as much objects of desire for these poems as lovers. For Gospodinov 'Language is ecstasy'.

Mark Robinson

ЕДИНАДЕСЕТ ОПИТА ЗА ОПРЕДЕЛЕНИЕ

I

то
тръгна отнякъде
(вече не помни началото)
трябва да стигне
(забрави къде)
и сега просто пътува

II

то
не е То за което си мислите
то
е нищото в стаята дето ви кара
да се обърнете рязко

III

то
е толкова малко с малко „т”
с меки уши и топли лапи
Никой още не го е виждал
и това е което доказва че
то съществува

IV

то
е силата с която
пада листа от дървото
в кофата вода

и размътва небесата

V

то
е също и покоя
в който силата се трупа
и небето се избистря

между две листа

ELEVEN ATTEMPTS AT A DEFINITION

I

it
started somewhere
(it doesn't remember where)
it has to get there
(it's forgotten where)
and now it just moves

II

it
is not the It you're thinking of
it
is the absence in the room that makes you
turn around suddenly

III

it
is so little with a little i
with soft ears and warm paws
no-one has seen it yet
and this is what proves
it exists

IV

it
is the flow that makes
the leaf fall from the tree
into a bucket of water

and blurs the sky

V

it
is also the stillness
that expands
and the sky clears

between two leaves

VI

Има нещо общо
в бръмбара и розата
и това е
то

VII

то
е в кръгчето на „о"
или между „т" и „о"
или дявол знае де е

но и дяволът не знае

VIII

Мислите че то е Бог
ала Бог
е с главна буква

IX

Казвате че е смъртта
Чуйте думите му само
        Смърт ли
вкусих я веднъж
беше кисела и твърда
цяла вечер плюх

X

то
е чезнещо и крехко
Назовеш ли го умира
Уловиш ли го си тръгва
и се стапя в празно-
то

XI

(и най-успешен опит)

VI

there is some connection between
the black beetle and the rose
and this is
it

VII

it
is in the dot of the i
or between the i and the t
or it's the devil knows where

but the Devil doesn't know

VIII

you might think it's god
but God
has a capital letter

IX

you might say it's death
but just listen to it
        Death?
I tasted it once
it was tough and sour
I was puking all night

X

it
is elusive and fragile
name it and it dies
catch it and it's gone
melting into emptiness

XI

(and the most successful attempt)

ЖЕНАТА НА ЛОВЕЦА

Жената на ловеца на жени
не издържа и хвана пътя
Брадяса
            омърлуши се ловеца
и дивечът си тръгна отегчен

ЛЮБОВ

Всяка нощ
да сънуваш жената
до която лежиш

БОГ

е сигурно щастлив
щом като си няма
Бог

ЗА СЪЧИНЯВАНЕТО

От жената съчинен е трубадурът
Мога да повторя пак
Тя е съчинила съчинителя
                        Гаустин от Арл, XII в.

Време е и аз да се измисля,
защото кой ще ме измисли някога.
Смъртта на циганките, дето ще ме хвалят,
И други приказки ме карат да побързам.

Измисли си, казват, някаква жена,
Другото, мъжът, е женска работа.

И ето я, тя вече съчинява
според страстта си мъжкото ми тяло,

THE HUNTER'S WIFE

The wife of the man who hunted women
couldn't bear it and hit the road.
The hunter lost it
            let his beard grow.
and the game drifted away, bored.

LOVE

Every night
to dream of the woman
who lies next to you.

GOD

must be happy
if He has no
God

ON INVENTION

> *It is woman who invented the troubadour*
> *I'll say it again:*
> *She invented the inventor*
>   Gaustin of Arles, XII century

It is time for me to invent myself,
for who else would ever invent me?
The gypsy women meant to praise me are gone –
thoughts like that make me hurry.

All you need to do is invent a woman,
the rest – the man – she'll take care of.

So off she goes, her passion invents
my male body,

тя съчинява двете ми ръце
опипващи и тежки,
тя съчинява белия ми дроб
и всяка алвеола поотделно,
и учестения ми дъх,
тя съчинява онова огромното
(така го съчинява тя – огромно).

Какъв замах! Тя съчинява!

И ето ме измислен, съчленен,
красив по своему, в една
приятна възраст, съблазнителен,
преди да съм измислил края.
А краят трябва да е тъжен
И да е хубав същевременно.

И аз измислям своя край:
Дали да свърша между пръстите
на най-добрата ученичка,
тъй както ме преписва, небрежна в правописа,
дали да свърша сам,
или изобщо да не свършвам,

защото кой ще ме измисли след това.

ЛЮБОВНИЯТ ЗАЕК

Ще се върна след малко, каза,
и остави вратата отворена.
Вечерта беше специална за нас,
върху печката къкреше заек,
беше нарязала лук, кръгчета моркови
и скилидки чесън.
Не си взе връхната дреха,
не сложи червило, не питах
къде отива.
Тя е такава.
Никога не е имала точна представа
за времето, закъснява за срещи, просто

invents my two hands,
heavy and groping,
invents my lungs,
each and every alveolus,
my quickening breath,
invents my giant part
(that's how she designs it – giant).

Such vision! Such imagination!

So here I am alive, newly created, complete,
attractive in my own way,
a good age, seductive,
before I invent the dying fall.
For endings should be sad.
And beautiful.

So I invent my own:
should I die between the fingers
of a straight A schoolgirl,
as she copies me down in a careless scrawl,
or do it on my own?
Should I even die at all,

for who would reinvent me then?

THE LOVE RABBIT

I'll be back soon, she said,
and left the door open.
It was a special night for us,
a rabbit was simmering on the hob;
she'd chopped onions, sliced carrots
and crushed garlic.
She wasn't wearing a coat,
she hadn't put her lipstick on, and
I didn't ask where she was going.
She's like that.
She's never had much sense
of time, late for everything, and that's all

така каза онази вечер –
Ще се върна след малко,
и дори не затвори вратата.

Шест години след тази вечер
я срещам на друга улица,
и ми се струва уплашена,
като някой, който се сеща,
че е забравил ютията включена
или нещо такова…

Изключи ли печката, пита тя.
Още не съм, казвам,

тези зайци са доста жилави.

HEY JUDE, 7 '09"

> *"Хей Джуд" е най-дългото бавно парче на света и ако за това*
> *това време не успееш да свалиш една жена, си най-смотаният*
> *мъж във Вселената.*
>
> Гаустин, VI в клас

Най-дългото парче, което пускахме,
траеше точно толкова: 7'09".
7 минути и 9 секунди
с ръце наелектризирани
от мохера на пуловера й.
7 минути и 9 секунди
за най-бляскавата история.
7 минути и 9 секунди
свят да ти се завие
и вие,
и все пак вие
се въртите,
и все пак тя се върти
около теб,
и все пак се върти
7 минути и 9 секунди.

she said that night,
I'll be back soon –
she didn't even close the door.

Six years later
I meet her in the street,
and she seems a little alarmed,
like a woman who's remembered
she's left the iron on
or something…

Did you turn off the cooker? she asks.
Not yet, I say,

rabbits are tough.

HEY JUDE, 7' 09"

> *It's the longest slow track ever and if you can't score
> with a woman in that time, you are the biggest loser in
> the Universe.*
>
> Gaustin, Grade VI c

It's the longest track ever,
just that: 7'09".
7 minutes and 9 seconds,
your hands electric
with the mohair of her jumper.
7 minutes and 9 seconds,
for your most glamorous story.
7 minutes and 9 seconds,
you are dizzy,
it's hard to believe
but you are spinning around,
it's hard to believe and yet she does move
around you,
yes, she is spinning around.
7 minutes and 9 seconds.

Никога след това,
никога по-късно,
и изобщо никога
(но тогава не знаеш)
няма да бъдеш толкова дълго
влюбен в една жена.

НОВИНИ

Тя затваря вестника и казва:
чете ли, в Айова
паднал град – парчета
като топките за голф.
Така е, казвам аз, защото
там прекаляват с голфа,
изгубили са много топки
и те сега се връщат,
Той им връща топките,
нали разбираш, Оня шегаджия.
Но тя не се засмива,
извръща се и казва ужасена:

Той винаги улучва.

ЧАЙ СЪС СМЕТАНА

На Т. С. Елиът,

il miglior té

Какво правиш, пита. Лека
английска утрин, казвам. Чета
Елиът, слушам Beatles. О,
казва тя, как ги смесваш?
Като сметаната с чая, казвам.
Като чай със сметана,
поправя ме тя, все пак Елиът
толкова много държеше

Never again,
never at all,
(though you don't know it yet)
will you be in love
with a woman
for this long.

NEWS

She folds the newspaper and says:
you heard the news from Iowa?
It hailed – hailstones
the size of golfballs.
Yes, I say,
they play golf all the time there,
they've lost so many balls
and now the balls are coming back.
Don't you see,
He is returning all their balls,
the Great Jester.
She is not amused.
She turns to me in terror:

He never misses.

TEA WITH MILK
  For T. S. Eliot

  il miglior té

How's it going, she asks. A gentle
English morning, I say. Reading
Eliot, listening to the Beatles. Oh,
she says, how do you mix the two?
Like milk with tea, I say.
Like tea with milk,
she corrects me, after all Eliot
really insisted

да бъде горчив и английски.
И си мреше по порцелана,
по вечерните вестници,
по звъна на лъжичките. Той
беше чаят, той беше чаят... Ония
бръмбари просто обраха каймака.

ПЧЕЛА

се бие о стъклото
о стъклописа със изкусно
изрисуваните лилии
от час
не е събрала грам прашец
ще се убие
пчелата на изкуството

SUICIDE

(фотография на Russel Sorgi, 1942)

Това е снимка от 42-а, Ню Йорк, не помня
номера на улицата, на преден план
е кафенето на хотела, отвън на тротоара
три кръгли маси, на четвъртата
пред чашите с кафе спокойно пушат
единствените двама посетители,
наоколо е пусто,
и ако вдигнат поглед в този миг,
ще видят там
(за нас това е центърът на снимката)
между деветия и осмия етаж,
като муха, като дефект на фотографията
жена,
която
пада.

on being intense and English.
He would kill for porcelain,
for the evening papers,
for the tinkle of teaspoons. He
was the tea, he was the tea… Those
beetles just lapped up the cream.

A BEE

keeps hitting the glass
the stained glass with
the finely painted lilies
it's been an hour
and not a speck of pollen
it will kill itself
this bee of art

SUICIDE
(a photograph by Russel Sorgi, 1942)

This is a photo from the Forties, New York – the number of the street
escapes me. In the foreground
there's a hotel cafe, three round tables
outside on the sidewalk, and at the fourth
the only two customers, cups in front of them,
idly smoking.
It's deadly quiet
and if at this moment the two look up
they will see
(for us this is the centre of the photo),
between the ninth and the eighth floor,
like a fly, like a smudge on the print,
a woman
falling.

Според историята, фотографът,
стажант в „Buffalo Courier Express",
бил там случайно, за да снима
ленив септември в Ню Йорк, пуста улица
и да я кръсти „2 следобед" или „Скука".
Но ето как нещата се променят,
заглавието става друго,
жената влиза в кадър – звезден миг
без никакво значение за нея
и все пак тя е жива
на фотографията
между деветия и осмия етаж,
страхът е в тялото, викът е в гърлото,
роклята е здрава и това
усилва ужаса.
Дори петната от кафе по тротоара
са още в чашите.

ФОТОГРАФИЯ II

Познавайки увлечението ти по анархизма в младежките години
и помнейки онова продънено куфарче с Бакунин, Кропоткин,
Щирнер („Единственият и неговата собственост"), все издания
на тогавашната библиотека „Безвластие", смея да ти предложа,
Гаустине, историята на още една семпла и без стойност за
другиго фотография от оня октомври в Сараево. Потроших цял
един ден да търся моста, където Гаврило Принцип, националист
и анархист ведно (любимо съчетание на Балканите), застрелва
от упор Австроунгарската империя в лицето, по-точно в гърлото,
на престолонаследника Франц Фердинанд през ранното лято на
1914-а. Имах неблагоразумието да разпитвам за това място
случайни сараевски граждани, които начаса ми хвърляха
кръвнишки погледи и отминаваха сякаш не са ме разбрали. В
самия край на деня някой се смили да ми укаже моста, който
съм щял да позная по изкъртената плоча на тоя „srpski peder".
И ето ме тук. Минавам предпазливо по отсрещния тротоар,
спирам се, прекалено нехайно паля цигара, а под якето стискам
заредена „Смяна", непретенциозна и безотказна машина, както
съм имал случай да се уверя. Леко потрепервам сякаш очаквам
всеки момент да избръмчи оттук автомобилът на самия Франц

The photographer, so the story goes,
was an intern on the *Buffalo Courier Express*.
He just happened to be there taking a photo
of a lazy September, an empty New York street,
meaning to call it 'Two in the Afternoon' or 'Boredom'.
But things change,
the title has to go –
the woman gets in shot, a starring role
which means nothing to her.
In the photo she is still alive
between the ninth and the eighth floor –
a cry in the throat, fear in the body –
her dress is intact, and that
shocks us all the more.
The coffee stains on the sidewalk
are still in the cups.

PHOTOGRAPH II

Remembering our youth, dear Gaustin, and your enthusiasm for anarchism, and that broken little suitcase with the works of Bakunin, Kropotkin, Stirner – all Anarchy Editions – I dare to offer you the story of one more photograph of that October day in Sarajevo – a simple photo of no value to anyone else. It took me a whole day to find the bridge where in the summer of 1914 Gavrilo Princip, a nationalist and anarchist (a favourite combination in the Balkans), shot at point-blank range the Austro-Hungarian Empire in the person of crown prince Franz Ferdinand. Or to be more precise, in the throat.

Unwise of me to ask passers-by for directions to the bridge – they all glared at me and hurried on as if they did not understand. Eventually a man took pity on me and told me to look for the bridge with a broken plaque commemorating 'that Serbian fucker'. So here I am. I cross warily to the pavement on the other side of the street and nonchalantly light a cigarette, a *Smyana* under my coat – it's simple but reliable, I've put it to the test many times. I am ready to shoot. I shiver, as if the car carrying Franz Ferdinand could whirr over the bridge any minute. Traffic goes by and a cold wind begins to blow. Right in the middle of this historic place, beside the broken plaque, an old man has laid out umbrellas for sale. Some of them are open. They

Фердинанд. Минават всякакви коли, излиза студен вятър. На историческото място точно под голямото петно от изкъртената плоча един старец продава чадъри. Някои от чадърите са разтворени и придават обем на картината, а и движение, защото вятърът започва да ги търкаля и старецът се опитва да ги укроти, настъпвайки ги за дръжките. Знам, че сега е моментът. Изваждам смяната, нагласил съм предварително блендата, и натискам спусъка. На снимката старецът е излязъл без глава, жертва на моята треперливост или на злощастното място, но циментовият парапет с липсващата плоча се вижда. Веднага след фотографическия ми атентат се намесиха Великите сили на облаците, както съм чувал да ги наричаш. Светкавичните телеграми, протестните ноти на гръмотевиците доведоха до бърза евакуация и опразване на булеварда. Последен се изтегли мокрият до кости продавач на чадъри.

Стоях под една стреха, на същото място, и изпитвах историческо чувство за вина. Спомних си всички убоги учебници по история, където се казваше, че надвисналите тъмни облаци над Европа само чакали искрата на онзи сараевски изстрел. Е, Гаустине, този ден над Сараево облаците наистина бяха тъмни. И фотографията го сочи, при това блендата е максимално отворена. Така стават големите бели. Просто някои нехайно подхвърлени метафори вземат, че се сбъднат.

Твой Г.

СВЕТОВНАТА ЕСЕН

Убедил съм се, че нямаме очи и уши, нито език за интригите и атентатите между Великите сили в Природата. Можем само да възклицаваме тази хармонична анархия.

Гаустин, *Ранни писма*

Тази година мога да кажа с точност
кога и къде свърши лятото.
Беше 24 октомври,
сряда, 6 и 40 следобед, Сараевско време.
Някой Гаврило Принцип
му пръсна от упор слънцето.
Беше си атентат, макар
да твърдят, че принципно
това се повтаря всяка година:

add volume and movement to the photograph: the wind is rolling them away and the old man is trying to stop them by standing on their handles. I know this is it, my moment has come. I take out the *Smyana* and shoot. In the picture the old man has no head – either my hands shook or this place is cursed – but the concrete rail with the broken plaque is there, in focus. Just as my deadly mission was completed the Great Cloud Powers – as you would call them – interfered. Lightning wired the news around and thunderclouds voiced loud protests, forcing me to retreat. The old man was the last to withdraw, soaking wet. I stood under some nearby eaves, sodden with historic guilt. I thought back to my idiotic history books, which said 'the bullet in Sarajevo was the spark that the dark clouds gathering over Europe were waiting for'. Well, my dear Gaustin, the clouds over Sarajevo that day were really dark. You can see how dark they were even though the photo is over-exposed. This is how big trouble comes about. Someone carelessly tosses up a few metaphors and they suddenly come true.

Yours, G.

GLOBAL AUTUMN

> *I know we have no eyes and ears, nor language for the intrigue and plotting of the Great Natural Powers. We can only marvel at their harmonic anarchy.*
>
> Gaustin, *Early Letters*

This year I can say precisely
when and where the summer ended.
It was the 24th October,
Wednesday, 6.40 pm, Sarajevo time.
A new Gavrilo Princip
shattered the sun point-blank.
It was all planned out, although
they say this happens every year
as a matter of principle:

студените западни фронтове,
антантите на циклоните,
крехки примирия, дъждове и депресии.
(Следват военните кореспонденции
на синоптиците.)

Така се започват Световните
есени.

ФОТОГРАФИЯ IV

Легендата към тази фотография, Гаустине, или по-точно нейната
география, накратко е следната. Представи си най-забутаното
северозападно кьоше на Гърция. На 5 часа от Солун, на три от
Козани и на час от Флорина. Точно тук, ще видиш по картата,
където се срещат Гърция, Албания и Македония, са двете
Преспански езера. Късно вечерта ни настаняват в бившата
гимназия на едно пустеещо селце. Строго варосани стаи с високи
тавани. На другата сутрин излизаме навън, август е и вече
напича, а ние с радост установяваме, че селцето е живо. Само
старци, ама живо. Оглеждат ни, без да се прикриват, както се
прави това само на Балканите, сетне идат при нас и ни
поздравяват на език, който няма да чуеш на друго място.
„Калимера, ко прайте?" Това казаха, Гаустине, вярвай ми, и като
видяха опулените ни физиономии, запитаха: „Нашенски знайте
ли?" Точно така, „нашенски". Усетих се благ и разтопен, като
един филологически Колумб. Защото нашенски ще рече особен
петмез от гръцки, сръбски, български, турски, македонски...
Чудех се, Гаустине, дали това е езикът отпреди Вавилон, или
един каращисан наново след балканските вавилонии говор.
Всичко това, сещаш се, не излиза на фотографията.

Антарктико се казваше селцето, което ще рече "бунтовно", а
тези мили старци-бунтовници се оплакваха, че албанците
прескачали баира на няколко пъти, бастисвали църквата и крадяли
кокошки от дворовете им.

Знам, че вече тръпнеш да научиш нещо за жената на снимката.
Хубава е, нали, и не прилича да е тукашна. Габриела, около 35-
годишна, играла на Бродуей, балерина и австрийка в едно.
Минала по тези места преди 3 години, харесало й, зарязала всичко
и останала. Сама, ако не броим онова страховито куче, което

cold Western fronts,
cyclones in alliances,
fragile truces, rain, depressions.
(Coming next: war reports from weathermen.)

This is how Global Autumns
                              begin.

PHOTOGRAPH IV

The key to this photo, my dear Gaustin, lies in its geography. Imagine the far north-western corner of Greece, five hours from Thessalonica, three from Kozani, an hour from Florina. This is the area of the two Prespan lakes – where Greece, Albania and Macedonia meet. We arrive late at night and they put us up in a former school in the deserted village. Stern whitewashed walls and high ceilings. In the morning we go for a walk. It's August, the sun is out, and we are glad to see that the place is alive. There are only old people around, but it's alive. They stare as if they know us, the way only Balkan people do, and they come up and welcome us with words you won't hear anywhere else. 'Kalimera, ko praite?' That's just what they said, Gaustin, believe me. When we stared back they asked: 'You speak our tongue?' That's right, 'our tongue'. My heart melted, I felt like a kind of linguistic Columbus – 'our tongue' meant this peculiar mishmash of Greek, Serbian, Bulgarian, Turkish and Macedonian… I wondered, Gaustin, if this was the language from before Babel or some new hybrid coming out of the Balkan hullabaloo. Needless to say, you can't see this on the picture.

The place was called Antarctico, which means 'rebellious' in Greek, and these dear old rebels complained to us that the Albanians come across the hills nearby, desecrate their church and steal hens from their backyards.

I know you are dying to hear about the woman in the picture. Good looking, isn't she? And obviously not from round here. Gabriela, 35, worked on Broadway. A dancer. And Austrian. She came to visit 3 years ago, liked it, and stayed, leaving her life behind. She was on her own, if you don't count that evil-looking dog in the lower left-hand

виждаш в долния ляв ъгъл. Тази жена, Гаустине, беше живяла на невероятни места, но през четирите вечери, докато пиехме с нея рицина отвън, на проста дървена маса под едрата гръко-албано-македонска луна, тя се държеше така, сякаш това забутано селце в най забутаната част на Балканите е центърът на света. А Медисън Скуеър Гардън, Бродуей и Виенската щатсопера се умилкваха като изоставени котета под масата, давайки мило и драго да бъдат около нея. Има минути, когато усещаш, че центърът на света е нещо много леко и подвижно, нещо като куче, подмамено от жена. Не искам и да си помисля, какво се случва с местата, които е напуснала. Сигурен ли си, че Австрия още съществува?

А кучето й, Гаустине, нито веднъж не изръмжа срещу мене.

Твой Г.

КУЧЕТО НА ГАБРИЕЛА

Баща му е сръбска овчарка
майка му – албанска хрътка
Единият му дядо – българска каракачанка
Другият по майчина линия идва от Солун
Мелезът на Балканите – смее се Габриела
(тя е австрийка с майка унгарка)
Не се бои от гърмежи
добро е за лов
ближе ръцете на всички
не се сърди ако му викаш
само понякога само понякога
(много рядко обаче)
се хвърля и хапе хапе...

corner. She'd lived in the most amazing places in the world, Gaustin, but the four nights we spent drinking retsina on the wooden table under the Greek-Albanian-Macedonian moon, she behaved as if this most distant of distant Balkan places were the centre of the universe. Madison Square Garden, Broadway and the Vienna Statsopera all rubbed against her feet under the table like abandoned kittens, begging for her company. Have you ever had moments when the centre of the world feels like something very light and agile, like a dog that's following a woman? I don't even want to think about what happens to the places she has left behind. Are you sure Austria is still there?

And her dog, Gaustin, it never once growled at me!

Yours, G.

GABRIELA'S DOG

His father is a Serbian shepherd
his mother an Albanian greyhound
his father's line is Bulgarian Karakachani
his mother's pedigree Thessalonican
he is a Balkan mongrel, Gabriela jokes
(she is Austrian, her mother Hungarian)
he is not afraid of gunshots
he is a good hunter
he licks everyone's hands
he won't be cross if you shout at him

sometimes just sometimes
(very rarely though)
he will jump up and bite and bite...

MARK ROBINSON

ELEVEN ATTEMPTS AT AN EXPLANATION

It is good to feel like a small child again, with your finger under each letter of a simple word. The sense of achievement at reading a streetsign before you are driven past it.

It is good to be reminded that many of our British practices are not universal.

It is good to have to think again in the first 15 minutes of collaboration.

It is good to be able to improvise once you have planned ahead and abandoned all your plans.

It is good to be able to go away and think. And then to think again.

It is good to have many, many words at your disposal and to try them all one after the other, as if they were keys to a door. Often the lock is invisible. And the door. That doesn't mean you can't open it. Or that you will.

It is good to make new friends and find you have new histories and can borrow tropes and trials as if they were trousers. That doesn't mean they will fit you, but it can be fun trying things on.

It is good to travel, but remember all travel happens within language and it's handy to have a translator to whisper in your ear.

It is good to be reminded what a strange and foreign place home is.

It is good to laugh when you are trying to remake a poem in a tongue it wasn't born in. Laughter can show you things the dictionary cannot.

It is good simply to make things with other people, whether that is music, dances, new rules for pool, performances, poems or fools of yourselves. It is what human beings do.

1300 MONUMENT SOFIA

So that it can rain Sofia turns inside out,
matt grey, nap smooth, flush with threat.
The fog has lifted, murk revealing dark.

The cast iron rifles of old Russian heroes
are falling bit by slow bit to the ground,
to lie at the foot of this gun-metal mountain

as the taggers of Levski ascend to fame.
They have new poetry to make that's beyond
old women marching trolleys across the square

after arm-crossed days in tiny shops
watching the stock gather silent dust.
All that musty patience flips the city right.

It is going to rain, and so that it can,
things are going to have to stay like this a while.

BOTEV v LOCOMOTIV, MARCH 2005, ADDED HELICOPTERS

Where the teams are named
for poets and revolutionaries
helicopters have been known
to spray rosewater onto pitches.
In a hotel guarded by Porsche 4 x 4s
I saw the Plovdiv derby
turn into a riot with one push.
The keeper let slip his straight red fate,
would not depart, the fans
and his teammates in a row
that grew like evening rain.
The fat little ref was simply lost,
did not know what he was doing.
Rubble showered the touchline.
In the centre circle all he could do
was twist the red and white band
on his wrist, neutral between yellow
and black and white, wonder
what he had done to offend

Grandma Baba Marta
halfway up the terrace,
a rock in her hand, singing
something rude about his father
until the helicopters arrived.

ESPERANTO ANONYME
for Bill Herbert, il lista-creatore migliore

Esperanto na billiardo
Esperanto de statistico
Esperanto of CNN
Esperanto of Chelski and Arsenal
Esperanto ah morning coughs
Esperanto of showerheads
Esperanto da breakfast buffet
Esperanto di bus
Esperanto of football stadia
Esperanto ye barking dogs
Esperanto a empty buzzwords
Esperanton a dead paradigms
Esperanto o't smoking gun
Esperanto of silence
Esperanto di iambs
Esperanto na ragged dance
Esperanto von fear
Esperanto o panic
Esperanto da drum and basics
Esperanto a hips
Esperanto na breath
Esperanto di grafiti
Esperanto de puzzled brows
Esperanto na hope
Esperanto ov hope over experience
Esperanto of beer
Esperanto of lists

RETURN

It is better to be in love with your wife
than to be in love with your poetry.
                    Toma Markov

1.

air like a lump in the throat
in this dark-haired city
if a horse could lay pumpkins
they'd be like those piled high
on market stalls at Sitnyakovo
and I'd be full of ginger carrying
my swollen heart home to bake

2.

This is a long fever, secret like a wish,
pale as you and flowers in its miracle heat.
It is close to mute, and lies snug in our palms in the dark.

So quietly new is it even now a breath might break
to talk of heart, hope, and then hold still
while our blood runs hot again,

guessing how every dry afternoon would feel
if this flush didn't warm the air,
didn't catch us falling into balance.

3.

Of many parallel worlds
I choose this one.

WHEN THE BEES ARE GATHERING HONEY
(ZigZag Trio)

1.

When the bees are gathering honey
a clarinet will tipsy over the brow
chased by an accordion. It will angle
through the undergrowth till it taps
blunt nose against rock.
It will spiral vexed over screes
of goatskin and whittling wood,
throw dirt behind its back.
Dazed, it will cramp suddenly
when it sees the sunlight,
flitter knuckled song to heavens
it squints to deeper hues,
so that it can finally breathe again.
It will make its way into the open
and wait for us to form lines around it.
It will tell us they should be circles.

2.

Downstairs, neat young men see us right
for crazy wedding jazz, downstairs
and left into a Cyrillic photograph
where you listen with your eyes, not your hands.
They will describe anything to you,
they say. It is better that way.
I think this is about saving yourself
for a wedding night which may not come.

3.

When I have finished dancing
I will hang a sheet from the window,
covered in honey and rosewater.
Then I will wait for the cowbells.

RE-ENTRY BLUES

On returning to work at the Arts Council after a week of performances in Sofia, October 2003.

When I woke up this morning I was feeling no pain.
But I drove me to Darlo and got on the train.
I headed for London and as I drew near
I thought 'bout the time that I'd had in Sofia.

Got the walking talking
corporate bend blues

I don't know what I'm doing but I do what I gotta,
Just like in rehearsals way up Mount Vitosha
Where Bluba Lu jammed and we poets studied rhyme
And something came out under pressure of time.

But now I got the walking talking
suited booted
corporate bend blues

I'm a profit agnostic and don't give a damn,
But half the North East thinks that I am The Man
Who makes arts decisions and dishes out dough,
Though deep in the Balkans they know it's not so.

I got the walking talking
Suited booted
Jargon-busting
Corporate bend blues

Though off to this really exceptional meeting,
to iambs and pulses my head is still beating.
The train speeding there rattles Sofia away
And gives me three hours to think what to say.

I got the walking talking
Suited booted
Jargon-busting
Arts transforming
Corporate bend blues

I could be sticking words to beats somewhere near Boyana
Instead I'm playing jargon bingo eating a banana,
All I need's a mention of building my capacity
And someone here will get to taste my vigorous tenacity
For making words jump and dance around the table
Seven days of Bulgar blues tell me that I'm able
To pull it out the bag and fill the air with lines –
But while meetings are a drag they also feel like mine…

So I take the damned tube right back to Kings Cross,
kidding myself 'bout the gain and the loss.
A small step forward, not one great leap.
By Newark North Gate I am sound asleep.

I got the walking talking
Suited booted
Jargon-busting
Arts transforming
Double meaning
Plain English speaking
Corporate bend blues

PHOTO:AUTHOR'S ARCHIVE

NADYA RADULOVA
Introduced by Linda France

NADYA RADULOVA's poems, like short beautifully-made films, are strong on mood and colour, peopled by intriguing characters in evocative settings. Their subject is the mysterious dance between the interior life and the exterior life, Self and Other, desire and the sadness that seems to follow in its wake.

The poems reveal a tender, sensuous relationship with the world and the people in it. There is a child-like wonder and appreciation of even the most mundane details of domestic life – the fridge and its contents in 'White Goods for Lovers' and the potatoes in 'The Small Rembrandt'. Decorating the Christmas tree in 'Fairy Lights' is a perfect image of this delight and freshness, with the added edge of a more adult electricity. Everything is surprising, miraculous, and reminds the reader of the beauty and joy in the simplest pleasures.

Hers is very much a woman's voice, asserting the importance and value of the home and relationships as suitable subject matter for a poem. This is a quiet, confident feminism, free of anger and blame and the impact is all the more powerful; particularly when viewed in the context of the establishment in Bulgaria. Radhulova's lyrics are braver and more radical than they may seem to Western readers.

Gender issues play an important part in Radulova's work as poet, prose writer, translator, academic and editor of *altera*, a vibrant magazine promoting a woman's-eye view of culture.These poems are marked by a distinctive rhythm, with the sense of ebbing and flowing, like the tides. Her most frequently-used device is repetition and this intensifies the effect of chant, a woman's voice singing, the Black Sea behind her.

Linda France

РУСКИ ПАМЕТНИК

там тя ескрила магдалените на пруста
и вишните и вишните на чехов
също бисквитките със битер-шоколад
в неделното легло на доктор лахневич

тъй както крие синия тайор
и шемизета с копчета коприна
по който връщат се прииждат връщат се
целувките във фолио от сняг

някъде в центъра на софия продава се
зад земеделската палата се продава
по северната стълба пруски свод
после на третия етаж отляво

непреходен тристаен изток
с няколко пукнати ребра
вроден порок
и туберози в двата дроба

я памятник себе воздвиг нерукотворний

а иначе там тя е скрила

а иначе продава се продава се

но също връщат се прииждат
връщат се

ЛАМПИЧКИ

Ако това стихотворение влезе някога в книга, то ще застане към края й – подобно коледно дърво в последните дни на декември, хиляда осемстотин осемдесет и втора година, когато била изобретена първата гирлянда електрически лампички.

моят любим
ме украсява в средата на стаята
памук стъкло и електричество
памук

RUSSIAN MONUMENT
For Nadya and her aunts

She has hidden proust's madelaines away
and the cherries, chekhov's cherries
and the dark chocolate biscuits
in dr. lahnevich's sunday morning bed

her tailored blue suit too
with that silk-buttoned chemise
all those kisses foiled in snow
ebbing back and forth and back

somewhere central sofia for sale
for sale behind ministry of agriculture
take northern staircase prussian vaulting
third floor apartment private entrance on left

three eastward facing chambers
a few broken ribs
innate valvular disease
and tuberoses in both lungs

No hands have wrought my monument

but otherwise she's been hiding

otherwise it is for sale for sale

but also they keep ebbing back and forth and back

FAIRY LIGHTS
For Leonid

This is a poem to stand at the end of a book, like a Christmas tree in the
last days of December 1882, when electric Christmas lights were
invented.

my sweetheart
is decorating me in the middle of the room
cotton glass and electricity
cotton

стъкло
и електричество
а после заедно двамата възпяваме
електрическото тяло

възпявам електрическото тяло:

аз съм направена от малки стъкълца
аз мъркам боцкам и жужа
и всички жички водят към
огромното ми стъклено сърце
сто свещи

моят любим ме включва
и изключва ме включва и
изключва

аз мъркам боцкам и жужа
а-змъ-рка-мбо-цк-ами-жуж-а
а по веригата се стича любовта
на малки глътки

играта продължава докъм полунощ когато
останат само реотаните
мокри оголени до златно нажежени
се вият около любимия ми който
продължава да включва и изключва да
включва и
изключва

докато гръмнат реотаните
и бъде светлина

glass
and electricity
then we sing
the body electric

I sing the body electric:

I am made of tiny pieces of glass
I purr prickle and buzz
and all the wiring leads
to my huge glass heart
one hundred candles bright

my sweetheart turns me on
and off and
on and
off

I purr prickle and buzz
I p-urrp-ri-ck-le-and-bu-zz
and love runs its circuits
in tiny mouthfuls

we play till midnight
all that remains is the filament
wet naked golden-hot
it twines around my sweetheart
still turning me on and off
and on and
off

until the elements short-circuit
then there is light

БЯЛА ТЕХНИКА ЗА ВЛЮБЕНИ

Всичко започва с малко влажни капки
по стените,
размекване на амбалажните хартии
и ултразвуково процъцряне
в контейнера за лед.

После
позамирисват броколите
и уж добре замръзналото трупче
на пъпеша
съмнително въздъхва.

Ред е и на желирания телешки език
да близне пощурелия перчем
на соевите кълнове в салатата
останала от вчера.

И ето камерата горе вляво
затопля се затопля се затопля
и скоро ще постигне нужния
сърдечен тон.

Накрая сбира дъх хладилникът,
напряга всички волтове и реотани,
водите си изхвърля върху неизметения
под в кухнята.

Храната гние, любовта цъфти,
Животът, казват, тръгвал от водата.
Вечерята за двама се отменя.
и дълго няма да заспим —

от глад.

WHITE GOODS FOR LOVERS

It all starts with a few wet drops
at the back, paper bags going soft
and a supersonic cracking
in the icebox.

The broccoli gives off a faint smell
and the well-chilled corpse
of the melon
lets out a suspicious sigh.

Next the jellied beef tongue
licks against the beansprouts
who run wild
in the remains of yesterday's salad.

The freezer compartment on the left
is heating up heating up heating
pumping up to the necessary
heartrate.

The fridge takes a final deep breath,
strains every volt and muscle,
then breaks its waters
on the unswept kitchen floor.

Food rots, love blossoms,
life, they say, came out of the water.
Our dinner for two is cancelled.
And we won't sleep for a long time –

we are starving.

ЕДИСОН

досущ котка захапала малкото за вратлето
светлината ме влачи из цялата стая
докато жили издуят стените
и килимът изплюе своето вълнено синьо сърце

в къщата няма стопани
само желания:
да се измъкна от пола си
от лявата си половина
от последната си твърдина литературата

котката е къпина която гори в средата на стаята
там се сбъдват всички желания
без умора
и без да оставят ненужни следи

после котката спи под кревата
после отново танцуваме
сипвам мляко в паничката
даже млякото свети

за приятелка имам махарани от далечна страна

ДО ПОИСКВАНЕ

Пощенска картичка: фотографирани
осем жени
вадят лук на полето.

Мина месец откакто съм там с тях –
най-голямата награда
на която съм се надявала.

Полето е загоряла тава
а облаците над него перилен препарат
който не може да размекне загорялото.

Аз и останалите жени правим същото –
човъркаме загорялото картофено брашно
но то не излиза и не излиза.

EDISON

like a cat carrying her young by the scruff
the light drags me round the room
until the veins of the walls are blue
and the carpet spits out its woollen heart

there are no landlords here
only desires:
to slip out of myself
my sex
my last skin, literature

the cat is a burning blackberry bush in the middle of the room
where all desires are met
without end
leaving nothing behind

later the cat sleeps under the bed
later we dance again
I pour milk into the bowl
even the milk is glowing

my friend is a maharani from a distant land

POSTE RESTANTE

Postcard: a photograph of
eight women
pulling up onions in a field.

I've been with them there for a month now –
the best thing
I could wish for.

The field is a scorched baking tray
and the clouds above are soft suds
which cannot shift the burnt bits.

That's what we are doing, the women and I –
scraping at the burnt potato flour,
but it won't come off, it won't come off.

По пладне вече сме извадили
дузина кофи лукови глави –
обелваме ги и ги дъвчем цели
докато перилният препарат проникне вътре в очните ни кухини
и изкара оттам
сълзи на благодарност.

Спим в студени, задни коридори.

На леглото до мен лежи млада китайка
с гърди непоникнали соеви кълнове.
В кутийка под леглото тя отглежда щурци.
Когато температурите паднат под нулата,
тя вади щурците и ги пъха под ризата си –

за да не замръзнат гласовете им.

VICTORIA INN

треторазреден хотел на белгрейв роуд
от грамофона с фуния излиза кралица виктория
с рокля за първо причастие

отразена в стенното зацапано огледало
хотелиерката свежда очи
кашмирено сини очи под синята лампа
после дава въженце за скачане на виктория
и посяга към ключа за нашата стая

всяка вечер от година насам
трийсет и осем паунда включва все същото
изглед към задния двор
скъпо платени стенания от горните стаи
на закуска мюсли и сливово сладко
смяна на чаршафите сутрин
ала все същите нокти все същата кръв по чаршафите

By noon we've taken out
a dozen buckets of onions –
we peel them and eat them whole
until the soap gets in our eyes
forcing
grateful tears.

We sleep in cold corridors, below stairs.

On the bed beside me lies a young Chinese woman,
her breasts like soya beans.
In a box under the bed she breeds crickets.
When the temperature falls below zero,
she takes them out and holds them under her shirt

so their voices don't freeze.

VICTORIA INN

a third-class hotel on belgrave road
from a gramophone's horn queen victoria rises
in her first communion dress

blurred by the mirror on the wall
the receptionist lowers her eyes
cashmere-blue under a cool blue light
then she gives a skipping rope to victoria
and reaches for the key to our room

night after night for the last year
£38 for the same thing
a view of the back yard
expensive moans from the rooms above
muesli and plum jam for breakfast
a change of sheets in the morning
but the same blood on the sheets the same nails

ако някога просто се върнем случайно по пладне
ще видим виктория
по неглиже и състарена
възнак на софата слуша
грамофонната музика да излиза
този път някак хрипливо и на туберкули от
същата онази фуния

в тези редки случаи ти затваряш очите ми
и полека ме сваляш по стълбите към нашата стая
после ме слагаш да легна на студеното двойно легло
и целуваш ръцете ми
морави китки които някога някой връзвал е
сякаш с въженце за скачане

МАЛКИЯТ РЕМБРАНД

В огледалото отсреща
стара
отдавна непочиствана печка
с дървени въглища
и умивалник отдясно.

Върху черния лепкав котлон
три картофа
два големи и един по-малък.

Минават години
докато в умивалника тръгне
гореща вода.

Ръцете на майка ми стават
червени червени
и чисти

сред мазните съдове студ.

if one day we happen to come back at noon
we will find victoria
looking old in her negligee
draped on the sofa listening
to the gramophone music that rises
this time in tubercular phrases wheezing from
the same horn

if this happens you close my eyes
take me carefully down the stairs to our room
lay me on the cold double bed
and kiss my hands
these purple wrists that someone once bound
perhaps with a skipping rope

THE SMALL REMBRANDT

In the mirror
an old
long neglected
charcoal-burning stove
and a sink to the right.

On the grimy black hotplate
three potatoes
two big and one smaller.

It was many years
before the tap ran
with hot water.

My mother's hands turn
crimson crimson
and clean

among the chill of greasy dishes.

VINEA MEA ELECTA

той беше твърде малък
непокръстен
за мойте тридесет и няколко години

търсех го из двора
зад високите стобори
но виждах само кожата му да се стеле
и да съхне
необезпокоявана от слънцето

по нея паяци пчели и еднодневки
хвърляха тържествено секрета си
смоковницата пускаше дълбоки неприлични
сенки
а нискостеблени растения изгризваха
от стъклописа на корема му
най-праведните цветове

поисках го от майка му

уви
бил още твърде малък
непокръстен
за виното което си измислях
сред папратите влага прах
и срам

СТЪКЛО

един прозрачен мъж се счупи в нея
отчупи се парченце стъкълце
заседна вътре
и я нарани

бе неочаквана
необезопасена
любов с протъркан етикет и мръсно гърло
не бе достатъчно газирано
не бе достатъчно студено
не се римуваха бикините със сутиена

VINEA MEA ELECTA

he was too young
unconfirmed
for my thirty-something years

behind the high walls
I searched for him in the yard
but all I saw was his skin settling
and drying
untouched by the sun

spiders bees and mayflies
ritually spilled their secretions on it
the fig trees had deep indecent
shadows
and the low-lying creepers choked
the immaculate blossoms
of his stained-glass belly

I told his mother I wanted him

but she said
he was too young
unconfirmed
for the wine I was fermenting
among the damp dusty shameful
ferns

GLASS

a transparent man snapped inside her
a sliver of glass broke off
caught within
and wounded her

it was unexpected
unprotected
love with a faded label and a grubby mouth
it wasn't fizzy enough
it wasn't chilled enough
the knickers and bra didn't rhyme

подобно тези на митичната машинописка
от огнената проповед

не беше още
излязъл преводът на
естетическа теория на адорно
и те не знаеха че болката им също бива
нетотална
и нетъждествена

също не знаеха
как да проникват там където
стават взаимни рани
които никой не лекува

и затова навярно от незнание
той вади с устни стъкълцето
а тя задълго занемява
додето се калцира несъвпадането

сега той е нейната висока пеперуда
а тя е неговия бял равнец
разделя ги стъкло
направено от малки стъкълца

той вече няма да се счупи в нея
тя няма да се нарани
макар да прокървяват заедно
когато влязат посетители
и прочетат табелката:

това е безопасна инсталация —
не е любов
а още по-малко е изкуство
още по-малко е изкуство
още по-малко е изкуство

like those of the legendary typist
in the fire sermon

the translation of
adorno's aesthetic theory
hadn't been published yet
so they didn't know their pain could also be
non-total
and *non-identical*

they also didn't know
how to push through to where
shared wounds would open
no-one could close

perhaps that's why out of ignorance
he takes the sliver out with his lips
she falls silent for a time
until the discrepancy heals over

now he is her distant butterfly
and she is his wild yarrow
separated by glass
made from small splinters

he won't be snapping inside her any more
she won't be wounded
although they both bleed
every time visitors come
and read the sign

this is a safe installation
it is not love
and it's not even art
it is not even art
it is not even art

LINDA FRANCE

STAMPS OF BULGARIA

I

Let's say it's the same as thinking about the past, thinking about a place you've never been. You make it up, try to remember anything that might give you a clue, explain something you never knew so you might understand why the stamps were triangles with cats on and the capital was a woman's name spelled wrong. Like the past, you've lost its currency, customs and folklore.

The only way to settle it, to break with the past, is to go there, go to the place you've never been. Buy a ticket, consult the maps. When you arrive the weather will take you by surprise. Someone will come to meet you and hold you in their arms like a sister. You will politely decline the offer of the local firewater. You will be tired from your journey.

This is all you know and all you need to know. The past will no longer haunt you. You are in a different country where all your memories haven't happened yet, all your ghosts still to be born. The alphabet is a different shape. There is some doubt about East and West. Magnetic North has lost its force. Walk into the day. Explore.

II

Have you ever noticed how something previously unknown, when you start thinking about it, soon becomes manifest, recurrent and almost familiar? So when I think of Bulgaria, there it is; as if my mind were a mirror and a whole country is casting its reflection.

A friend's email tells me of a holiday romance with a Bulgarian doctor called George; people jumping out of bushes, offering to change sterling; the two phrases of Bulgarian her father learnt: 'Stars on 45' and 'I have a headache'. The last sentence iambic and thrilling – *And everyone wanted to buy your jeans.*

Unaccountably, in the newspaper there's a photo of *a Muslim bride from the village of Ribnovo.* Her face is painted white and covered in coloured sequins, flowers and sunbursts. Her headdress is decorated with artificial flowers and tinsel, a lammetta veil. The bride's eyes are closed as if she were dead.

On the radio I hear a programme about a wave of expats, attracted by the cheap houses, sick of living in England, which feels more and more, they say, *like trying to walk up a hill and never reaching the top*. In Bulgaria the worst that happens is a gypsy stopping them in the street, asking if they want to buy a baby.

III

I was wrong about the stamps. When I go back to my album, they are all rectangles. There is one empty row, smudged with the left-over adhesive of three hinges. Maybe these were the stamps with cats on. Otherwise it is aeroplanes and footballers – the 1966 World Cup. A woman on a horse. A woman playing volleyball.

There are a couple of two-tone photographs: one of a large impressive-looking dam in shades of turquoise; the other of juicy pears growing on a tree. This one is tinted red.

These are the colours of my childhood, slightly faded; indecipherable postmarks and rough perforations. I stare at the Cyrillic script, its backwards Bs and upside down Vs, as if I could breathe in their meaning. What I read there is that writing, in any language, is only a sign. I can choose to follow it but must remember it isn't where I am going.

IV

These past few months it feels as if my mind has slipped through my skull, down my spine, into the region between my shoulderblades, behind my heart. Easier for my mind to slip down than for my heart to climb up: we human beings so much at the mercy of gravity.

I'm trying to find the Bulgaria in my heart. The place it touches is the very spot that quickened when it heard someone say that in Bulgarian the words for time and weather are the same. A cool wind blew across the dusty plains and I knew there'd be rain. I found myself longing for mountains and a new language, fat and soft in my mouth, fresh as aubergines, yogurt, garlic and dill.

Time and weather are where my heart lives, machine for beginnings and endings that it is. At a certain time in certain weather, my heart and I shall fly to Sofia. We will eat our fill and everything will be uncertain, everything will change.

EAST

Bulgaria's capital city, the highest in Europe, is named after Saint Sofia, an aspect of the Wisdom Goddess, Sophia.

In order to arrive at what you are not
You must go through the way in which you are not,
And what you do not know is the only thing you know
And what you own is what you do not own
And where you are is where you are not.
                              T.S. Eliot 'East Coker'

I Hors d'oeuvres

Two hours I lost and gained two thousand miles,
the clock inside me counting them one by one,
nothing on my face but numbers.
                              Rising
so high above the clouds leaves you with a hunger
wide as Europe. You could eat a whole city
alive.
        And so I do, bite by bite, the taste
of it glinting in my mouth – yogurt, sharp
as snow; sheep's cheese brought to the table
sizzling with honey and walnuts; coffee's
esperanto froth.
                              Everything I order
is white, medicine swallowed from a saint's spoon.

I stir from dreams about feasting, almonds
splitting into two bleached halves, both for me;
a fresh reach of flavours in my bowl licked clean.

II Broken Music

Hope is one of the city's martyred daughters.
Her other name is Silence.
                              If I look up
I find her in the shell of autumn sky,
oak leaves golden in the Saturday park –

an egg hatching an arcane alphabet,
thirty letters singing their sounds under
my skin: 'zh' as in *azure*; the 'sh' in *she*;
the 'z' in *zero* and 'f' as in *far*.

I hear the lilt of her in the ballads
of the blind man outside the Metro,
the sunset call of the muezzin,
a busker tonguing *Yesterday* out of his sax.

And when I lift my head again – in the fizz
of sapphire fireworks from the tramwire's sparks.

III Nightology

In Passport Control the first thing I see –
a billboard for some nightclub telling me
So Daddy's dolls get undressed themselves.

Welcome to a city named after
a goddess, dressed in black, her gold face a mask.
She directs the traffic with her laurel wreath,
a dark doubting angel, while the women
walk through her streets as if they're carrying
heavy parcels.
                      In the market they try
to sell me mouse bait and pop sox. I buy
dried mushrooms, loving the curves of this earth.
They say it's Black like the Sea is.

It's only by night I notice the domes
of the churches shine like a mother's breasts.

IV OUTING

Here it's called a gypsy summer. The sun
strokes my cheek with a gaze it could never
get away with at home, shocking as vodka.

My walk's different too. I must fit my feet
to the rise of the cobbles, the winding lanes,
too aware of my thighs, my hips.
                                 I find
a printer's stamp on the stones – number 5 –
ink still wet.
                  Inside the museum house
I imagine I'm wearing a crimson dress,
fingers itching at the coarse weave behind glass,
the braid one woman stitched in the evenings
after days spent picking yards of roses.

I sit above the ruined theatre and sip
passion fruit juice, let the past stripped naked cool me.

V POLLINATION

What am I breathing in with this dusty air,
sultry at the flea market, the smell
of other people's lives laid out on tables?

So much moulded from metal – coins and medals,
badges with Lenin's face or swastikas,
enamelled prizes spelling *Perfect Home* –
the tang of blood no one wants to remember.

And always a cigarette smouldering
over my shoulder like a beacon
of lost faith.
                 I can't get the sadness of it
out of my nostrils;
                       inhale as much as I can
of the fragrance of plane trees, grass still green,
that woman's perfume – a hundred flowers in bloom
I track down the boulevard like a bee.

VI TREASURE

If Sofia has a sixth sense, it would
be a secret. The Romans passed down

their fear with their letters and roads, angry
with ghosts and doves, love and wisdom's milk.

I am child, I am mother in a palace
of mirrors, watching for what's hidden in

the spaces between things, what tarnished light
spills from the cracks – all I've forgotten I knew.

My last day I spot a ring of silver keys buried
in the pavement across from the Russian Church

where the women go to pray for miracles.
I hang one round my neck for what it might

unlock in me and, flying home, come to
the circus of my senses, ride the turbulence.

V B V
Introduced by W. N. Herbert

VBV the poet is not to be confused with the person Vassil B. Vidinsky: as he has mischievously pointed out, 'The biographies of both names are completely different and never interweave'. Vassil is an urbane European – formerly involved in advertising, an International Scholar in Belgium, he has recently completed a PhD at Sofia University. VBV, on the other hand, is attempting to renovate the Bulgarian language so that it can perform a startling series of cultural acrobatics. He looks at the interface between east and west with a profoundly historical sense of the fractures between Europe and Asia, and the particular role of the Slavic cultures of the Black Sea that have been caught between the two.

His poems are full of strange energies, straining at the limits of colloquial expression, but they also embody a lovely melancholic lyricism: he has explained that he likes to investigate 'old-fashioned experimental literature'. That deliberate use of apparent oxymoron, like the curious gap between Vassil and V, is key to an appreciation of his distinctive voice. Exuberant neologisms, departures from normal laws of punctuation or capitalisation, irruptions from Lithuanian, fictitious locations, recipes and relatives – everything is grist to the mill of a highly original eye and ear.

As you might imagine, his work isn't exactly an effortless breeze to translate, but the search for equivalent expressiveness in English, and the effort to translate his tactics as much as his language, have both been worth it to encounter this unique voice.

W. N. Herbert

A.

Своето като страшно;
Биволският език като сняг;
Курдисвам часовник на джамията,
Навивам чалма върху част от главата –
Ушните кухини стоят отвън,
за да слухувам.
Постилам черджето по локвите,
      (не мога да пея:
        затуй молитвата ми
        звучи като чуждински език…
        Лингвистите знаят кой.)
Накланям слънчогледите към земята.
Локвите като не-слънце.
И произнасям разнообразни звукосъчетания в глината
      и от бълбукането
      се потя:

ЮГОИЗТОК

…А сутрин имаше много ананас, имаше орехи в сочните ябълки,
      канела в греяното вино
и дълги листа тютюн в нашия чай от лешници и лек анасон.
      На обяд турунджавия мед от портокалите
        се стичаше в сочни смокини
        и ние пушихме сандалово дърво
        с капки гъсто борово мляко.
      На свечеряване слагахме червените грейпфрути
        в кани с горещ карамел
        и лягахме
        край зелените лимони на нощта,
      пиехме от тях дълги глътки ягодова сметана
        с цариградски бадеми
        и сочен тишпищил.
      А сред уханието на лененото семе и
        едрите маслини,
        големите нощни стафиди
        се топяха
        в устите ни
        като арменско бяло сладко
        преди да съмне джинджифила…

A.

Your own as threatening;
The buffalo tongue like snow;
I wind up a clock on the mosque,
I swathe a turban round part of my head –
the aural orifices remain outside
for me to earwitness.
I spread the mat over the puddles
        (I can't sing:
        hence my prayer
        sounds like an outlandish tongue...
        linguists know which one),
I bend the sunflowers towards the earth.
The puddles as a non-sun.
I utter various soundstrings under the clay
        and from the babbling
        I sweat:

NEAREAST

...in the morning there were loads of pineapples, there were walnuts in the juicy apples
the mulled wine was full of cinnamon
and long tobacco leaves floated in the hazelnut-and-star-anise tea.
At noon the amber honey from the oranges
oozed into softening figs
and we smoked sandalwood
with drops of thick pine-tree milk.
At dusk we placed pink grapefruits
in hot jugfuls of caramel
and lay down for the night
amongst green lemons
drinking long mouthfuls of strawberry cream
with Constantinople almonds
and syrupy tishpishti.
Amid the scent of linseed
and fat olives
big nocturnal raisins
melted
in our mouths
like Armenian white jam
until the ginger tree awoke...

ДЕТСТВОТО НА АРМЕНИЯ

Моята тънка черна баба изпълзя
усмихнато зад шкафа и на стената от червени тухли,
морска карта окачи.

– От дядо си лулата да запалиш и веригите
на крака си да увиеш. Чорапи ще ти изплета
от корабни платна и очила ще ти огъна
от стари телескопи.
– Бабо...

Очите ми са сложни, очите ми са дълги.
В тухлите ровичкам от дете и моливите там си
буча, листчета си крия.
Затворих шкафа да не тегли стаята надолу и
Баба си изпратих по дъските.
Обръщам се.
От картата морето ми изтича. По тухлите ми
                                        капе.
Черното море по моята стена.
Тъмно е морето –
                      капе.
По стената – само вадички и зъбери...
и някаква пердашена мазилка.
Морето всичкото ми детството ще залее...
Залее и заля – всички моливи изгниха,
а листата като салове се носят –
всеки с някаква история, скована от съгласни.
Тъй в Армения бабите внуците израстват –
носят им карти и
сол дълбоководна.
Солта е за очите, за да виждат.

– Ела, Йоханес...
И морето ми е до колене –
качил съм се на гърба на баба си.
Очите й са сложни, очите й са дълги,
ръцете – стари телескопи.
Излизаме от стаята полека.
А на вратата – восъчна табела:
„Домът е стара баба"

ARMENIA'S CHILDHOOD

My skinny black grandmother crawled out
from behind the cupboard with a smile and on the red-brick wall
hung a map of the sea.

"Light your grandad's pipe and wrap the chains
around your legs. I will knit you a pair of socks
out of sails and make you a pair of glasses
out of old telescopes."
"Grandma…"

My eyes are complex, my eyes are long.
I've poked at that brick wall since I was a child –
I stick my pencils in there, and hide my bits of paper.
I closed the cupboard so it didn't pull down the room
and crossing the wooden floor, saw my grandmother off.
I am turning around.
The sea is flowing out of the map. Down my brick wall
– dripping.
The Black Sea down my wall.
Dark is the sea –
dripping.
Down the wall – becks and outcrops…
through rough stucco.
The sea will overwhelm my childhood…
and so it did – my pencils rotted,
scraps of paper now floating rafts –
each with a history nailed together with consonants.
This is how grandmothers bring up children in Armenia –
they give them maps
and salt from deep waters.
The salt is so the eyes can see.

"Come, Yohannes…"

I know I can wade through the water –
I am on my grandmother's back.
Her eyes are complex, her eyes are long,
her hands old telescopes.
By and by we leave the room;
on the door a sign made of wax:
"Houses are old grandmothers".

B.

Въжетата, с които вързах моя син
са все още мокри и обтегнати.
Таванът е залостен с дървения шкаф,
а роклите висят обесени.

Редим одеколони по ъглите,
може би се грижим по войнишки.
И двамата сме се завърнали във София,
за да вържем с миналото нишки.

Надвесени сме над чугунената мивка,
в квартирата с евтиния порцелан.
Пред огледалото стоим в почивка;
и знаем - последно всеки се гримира сам.

Остарели сме и приличаме на братя –
както всъщност е било завинаги.
Привикнали, аз и моят син мълчим:
театрални, уморени и усмихнати.

ОСТРАНЕН ВЗГЛЯД

...колко е „Объркана" физическата ни География,
гледайки я от Молдова на Юг:
ние сме без *форма* (леко на Запад), „потни" –
Кавказка провинция с огромни спомени.
„Незабележими в левия морски ъгъл" – (Щ.)
(покатерени отвъд Дунава и затиснати Отгоре).
Как е различна Граматиката чута от предградията
на Кишинев и Кагул
(и още повече от „следградията" или ниските брегове
на Днестър) и как спрягаме глаголите си,
неспокойни и за Историята и за Геологията (ни),
вперили очни ябълки надясно, Яржидво.
(покачени; за да прехвърлим взором поне Алпите)
и после антропоморфни:
откриваме наново очуднения си landschaft –
като паломници
край черноморското затворено огледало-изход.
в гръб. в лице.

V.

The ropes I used to tie my son
are still tight and wet.
The wardrobe hides the attic door,
the hanging dresses swing.

We parade bottles of cologne,
we're back in Sofia at last,
two careful soldiers, maybe,
tying the threads of our past.

We are leaning over the cast-iron sink
in furnished quarters neither of us own.
We stand in front of the mirror and think:
in the end we put on our make-up alone.

We've grown old and look like brothers –
the way it's always been.
We are used to this. My son and I are silent:
theatrical, exhausted, smiling.

STRANGE VISTA

...how 'Confused' our physical Geography seems
when you look south from Moldova:
our country has no *shape* (we are slightly to the West), 'sweaty' –
a Caucasian province with gigantic memories.
'Unnoticed in the lefthand corner of sea' – X.
(scaled high up beyond the Danube and squeezed from Above.)
How different the Grammar sounds in
the suburbs of Kishinev and Kagul
(even more so in the sup:urbs or on the lower banks
of the Dnester) and how strangely we conjugate our verbs,
worrying about (our) History and geology,
eyes staring to the right, Yarzhidva.
(high up, so we can look beyond the Alps)
and then anthropomorphic,
we rediscover our miracled Landschaft –
like pilgrims
around the looking-glass of the Black Sea.
backwards. forwards.

Слизам от Молдова на Юг,
а отраженията ми навлизат към Киев –
само тук Днепър и Дунав се пресичат.

КАВКАЗЪ

(операционализъм)

Моят дом срещу моята крепост

Отвикнах.
Театърът е единственото старо хътърство (ars; art).
И тук, при осетинците Образьницата (historia) е театро.
(отдалеченост).
Ударенията върху предметите се изме(с)тват. И механични
предприятията се задвижват с Грамофони.
Всяко пред-приятие – песен.

I АЗЪРБАЙДЖАН - ПЕСЕН ПЪРВА

„Каруци след каруци, във всяка каруца по кораб – тумбести
дървени кораби… Удавници-говеда пасат.
Пасат и ми пеят…"
О, моя Родино – центробежните твои полета върху
                    мъртви биволици и трудни жени. С подложка –
Черен, меден Иран. Как да запазя органите ти от бягане
                                        и от подобие?
И най-големият Страх
– тук земята има Посока.

II АРМЕНИЯ – ПЕСЕН ВТОРА

„…той в шепа държи Църквата, а вътре се блъска народ.
И в същата длан – Арарат. Гората и обществото бяха едно.
Оставете ни сами. Оставете ни самотни."
…Но тук няма бесилки!?, и значи няма Уредби, няма надежда…
Историята е проста словоформа,

I head south from Moldova,
but my reflections march towards Kiev –
only here do the Dneper and the Danube meet.

THE CAUCUSES
(an operation)

'My home against my castle.'

I've quit.
Theatre is the oldest cunning (art).
Here amongst the Ossetians History become theatre
(remoteness).
The accents of objects shift. The mechanical factories
are started up by Gramophones.
Every factory a song.

I AZERBAIJAN – FIRST SONG

"One cart after the other, a ship in each cart – bulging
wooden ships… Drowned people grazing.
They graze and sing…"
Oh, my native land – dead buffalo and pregnant women
                                beneath your centrifugal fields.
And at the very bottom lies Black, copper Iran.
How can I save your limbs from flight

                                or idolatry?

And the greatest Dread here
– Earth has a Direction.

II ARMENIA – SECOND SONG

"…he is holding the Church in his palm, and inside it – human bustle.
In the same palm – Ararat. Forest and society used to be one.
Leave us alone. Leave us lonely."
…But there are no gallows here! That means there is no Order, no hope…
History is a simple word,

запазена в нервни стомах и уста.
Потомясан стърча, а у дома акварелът
                 е нетрайност на областта:
там е опасно, но Творкиня съм аз:
Стоя в място и чакам новия Модернизъм:
има Бог – и това са Другите...

III Грузия – песен трета

„Да остана бащиния без грузински очи и
да отметна, забравя – че само тук има стълбове до небето
и жици в пръстта. Проклет да съм тогава: Оставенец.”
Черно море е най-средиземното – то е Архив и ишлеме,
Единственият прилаз на глубоките византиуми
към Севера. Нашият усън – безполезната зирка.
А нощта тук е състояние на веществото:
ето – в-вото си изврьща полека утробата навън
     и в мрак Звуките попиват в телесното –
     всеки предмет(нат) със свой глас през нощта.

...Отвикнах, но се връщам.
В Кавказът ми. И ужасът от това, че има ехо.

БРЕМЕННИЯ ОФИЦЕР
(военен стенопис)

    'Ye shall know the Truth, and the Truth shall make you angry.'
                                Aldous Huxley

Аз нямам вече крайници и битки –
единствено тегло в корема и плътност във гърдите.
Притежавам стенописи във полето по наследство:
Нека спрем пред първия от тях.

I stand out, lost, while at home the watercolours
                         show the mutability of the field: it is
dangerous there, but I am a Creatress:
I take my place and await the new Modernism:
God exists – and God is Other people...

III GEORGIA – THIRD SONG

"To stay in my native land and lose my Georgian eyes,
and to forget, to leave behind electric posts as high as skies
and copper wiring in the ground only here, only here.
Let me be cursed then – a stuck-in-the-dirt."
The Black Sea is the most mediterranean – it is an outsourced Archive.
The only way for deep byzantiums
to reach the North. Our deep sleep is a useless hole.
And the night here is a physical condition:
matter slowly turns its womb inside out
    and in the dark the Sounds sink into the body –
    each Object with its own voice in the night.

...I've quit, but I am coming back.
To my Caucuses. To the fear of an echo.

THE PREGNANT OFFICER

(a military mural)

'Ye shall know the Truth, and the Truth shall make you angry.'
                                        Aldous Huxley

I no longer have limbs and battles
only a weight in my belly and a thickening in my breast
my legacy is painted walls in the field:
let's stop before the first.

Първи

Войската тежко, необходимо се оттегля –
зарязани в полето ранените войници раждат:
така е
в края на всяка битка.

Затова войниците предварително понесоха
множество съоръжения, предмети:
за музика, за звук, за тон, за отмет.
В полето да направят сватби.
Нарамиха цели уреди и домакинства.
И на сражение заминаха преди година.
Войниците възседнали угоените си крави
с копия пробождаха
нервната почва и плътния тор.
Вече трудни, но в разгара на войната.

40 седмици в полето се трудиха с жертви.
И в битката построиха сгради – за да се утъпче пръстта,
за да се отложи тежката глина.
За да изпръхне полето като пяна.
Та тук има толкова способности и скътана земя
в излишък.
…
…

Аз нямам вече крайници и битки –
нищо във корема, нищо във гърдите.
Притежавам стенописи, които не желая.

Втори

Зарязани в полето ранените войници раждат:
дечицата излизат и баща си търсят.
Търсят – но полето е огромно.
Търсят – и всички са бащи.
…

FIRST

The army ponderously, unavoidably withdraws –
abandoned in the field wounded soldiers give birth:
that's how it is
at the end of battles.

That is why the soldiers armed themselves beforehand
with a mixture of implements and tools:
for music, for sound, for register, for checking off.
To conduct weddings in the field.
They shouldered whole inventories and households.
And went to the front a year ago.
The soldiers, riding their fattened cows,
pricked with spears
the nervy soil and the thick manure.
Already heavy, but in the heat of battle.

40 weeks in the field they laboured, with casualties.
In the midst of battle they erected buildings – to impact the soil,
to leach the difficult clay,
to dry the field like foam.
There are so many resources – and land tucked away,
more than enough.
...
...

I no longer have limbs and battles
nothing in the belly, nothing in the breast
I own murals I don't want.

SECOND

Abandoned in the field wounded soldiers give birth:
children appear and look for their fathers.
They look – but the field is enormous.
They look – and everyone is a father.
...

А после идват бавно
тежките семейства
и дългите роднини –
идват да закусят,
краката да обтегнат,
карти да играят.
Карти и съдби да подредят.

ДВЕ МЪЖКИ ПРИКАЗКИ

Мъжете винаги искат.

: да бъдат главни герои – да висят със
страшна сила към Земята. Затова играят
карти, пият спирт и разказват мръсни вицове.
И всеки един има война в задния си джоб.
Изневяра в панталона.
И детство пълно с пирати.

Ала няма филми за толкова герои,
нито режисьорки, които да им вярват.

И на – нямото кино се пренася
по строежите и масите.
Защото каквото и да кажеш – все едно
не си го казал.
И за целия живот – ни една
запомняща се реплика.

Затова мъжете стоят уморени по гарите
и чакат да ги викнат на фронта.
Мъжете пеят с гърло под масите
и чакат да ги приберат за бунта.
Мъжете стоят
и чакат със страшна сила…

Ала всъщност няма герои за толкова филми,
нито режисьори, които да си вярват.

Then here come, very slowly,
the extended families
and the distant relatives –
to eat breakfast,
to lounge around,
to play cards.
Deal out cards and fortunes.

MAN-TO-MAN

Men always want.

To be the hero – to swing from the gallows
with a terrible force towards Earth. That's why
they play cards, drink spirits and tell dirty jokes.
And each has a war in his back pocket.
Infidelity in his jeans.
And a childhood full of pirates.

But there aren't enough films to go round,
or women directors to make them.

And so – building sites and tables
turn into silent movies.
Because whatever you say – it's like
you never said it.
All your life, not even one memorable one-liner.

That's why tired-looking men sit in stations,
waiting to be called up.
Men under the table belting out songs,
waiting to be booked for mutiny.
Men who stay there
and wait with a terrible force...

In truth there aren't enough heroes to go round,
or film-makers who believe in themselves.

...и ни една запомняща се реплика,
освен последната:
"Такъв е животът..."

ВОЙНА

(обобщение на "Е:то.")

I ОТИВАНЕ НА ВОЙНА

Отивайки като войнстващ *с очила*
аз намервам жертвеници по полезрението на своя добитък
и с кон съм втурнат срещуположно на врага си
　　　　　с пушка с много резби и дръжки
защит:вам и защитавам зад дланта си не Родина, а себе.
Врагът ми е Културата.
　　　　　Хитър съм, умелотежък (*без тегло няма движение*)
　　　　　възпитан с вековити умения за лек срещу разбирането,
　　　　　　　　схващането.
Хващам, фъргам, пея – друсам си телесата – размахнат във
　　　　　　　　протяжност и всичко усявам...
На война като на война –
　　　　　Другото съм себе си.

II РАМКИТЕ ПРЕДИ ВОЙНАТА

За мен като воин: Най-много обичам Рамките
　　　　　　　　и желязото:
Ключалките ме подтискат.
Когато пипам дръжката на прозореца
усещам своя орган-ръка: гънките, дори извивката й.
Мисля, че пипането е повече от окото.
И пипайки Пирони и забивайки ги – ставам по-сглобен, Здрав.
Ето – Ръбовете възбуждат, но не половите ми органи,
а тези *за ровичкане и събиране:*
　　　　　　　　Ръбовете са времето.
　　　　　　　　Светлосенките са мястото.

… and not even one memorable one-liner,
except the last:
"That's life…"

WAR

(a summary of Th:is*)*

I THE GOING TO WAR

Going as a warmonger *in eyeglasses*
I pick out sacrificial altars within my cattle's field of vision
and I steer my horse away from the enemy,
            with an elaborately-chased rifle with many handles
I shield and field behind my hand not my native land but myself.
My enemy is Culture.
            I am cunning, heavybutdeft (*no mass no movement*)
            I was raised with ancient skills, a charm against understanding,
                        against awareness.
I grab, I lob, I sing – I shake my blubber – waving wildly
                        broadcasting far and wide…
All's fair in love and war –
            I am that which I am not.

II THE FRAMES BEFORE THE WAR

About me as a soldier: most of all I love Frames
                        and iron;
Keyholes depress me.
When I touch the window handle
I feel my hand as a thing, its wrinkles, even its curves.
For me, touching is deeper than seeing.
And groping for Nails, driving them home, I feel more assembled, Strong.
Look – the edges turn me on, but it's not a sexual thing,
it's in the *rummaging and gathering*:
            the edges are time
            the shading is place.

Но когато милвам веществото
и желая да го удължа се явява Войната.
И се изменя погледът и Костите ни,
с които гледаме.
Рамките, рамките!: *Защото съм иконоборец.*

III Условия за война

От всичко до тук и нататък изграждам своето сражение:
Пилея слуха си, за да има Обем. (в плоскости да
                                    воювам не умея)
Организирам метеорологични у:словия вместо
обстоятелства:
            (свръхкратките гласни
        да се чуват по средата на полето;
        по-нататък дългите;
        а към мене съгласните – защото всяка Дума е об(в)ласт)
И *пипам*, за да бъде войната тяло Божие.
                            И в него –
Войната е просто симбиоза и заместване.
Ставаме едно.
Ставаме 1.

IV Битката във войната

И напрежение завинаги:
Напрегнат ще! като телесно дърво… И тогава –
Изпънати мускулите ще се втвърдят до кости
            като печена глина в стомах на добитък;
Очите се издуват от напрежение
            и издадени *всичко ще виждат.*
И когато стискайки зъбите, те се набият във венците ми…
И слепоочията хлътват навътре;
            И притискат опънатото вещество.
И удължената ми кожа – с изпъкнали, отделени вени и жили.
И без мигли и вежди от напрежението…

И след продължителен напън мускулите ще са отровни.
И ноктите са органични – а това така боли.
            Така боли растежа.
Тогава, точно тогава: *Аз те обичам, мое момиче, мой навик и граница.*
Моя култура.

But when I caress substance
and seek to extend it, War arrives.
And alters sight and the Bones
with which we see.
The Frames, the frames! *All because I am an iconoclast.*

III CONDITIONS FOR WAR

From everything up to here and beyond I build my battle:
I splash out my hearing to claim Space (within surfaces
                                        I have no skill for war).
I organise meteorological condi(c)tions instead of
circumstances:
            (clipped vowels
        should be heard in the middle of the field;
        the longer ones further on;
        the consonants near me – because every Word is area(l)blast).
I *grope* so the war becomes the Body of God.
                            And in Him
the war is simply symbiosis and substitution.
We become one.
We become 1.

IV THE BATTLE IN THE WAR

And constant tension:
I shall be tense! Like a tree with limbs… And then
the taut muscles will harden into bone
            like fired clay in the stomach of cattle
the eyeballs are bulging with the tension
            and protruding *they shall see all.*
And grinding my teeth, their roots impale my gums…
And my temples implode;
            and compress the substance inside.
And my distended skin – with swollen veins and distinct sinews.
And lashless and browless from the tension…

And after protracted strain my muscles will be toxic.
And fingernails are still organic – this really hurts.
                    Growth really hurts.
At that moment, at that precise moment *I love you, my girl, my habit and border.*
My culture.

V Оглеждане след война

Ей го – на.
Когато се обърнах видях твърдото Черно море –
Трупове: толкова милиарди, огромни и разложени
                          тела не се вместваха
                          в моя кръго:зор –
Напънах се – и когато очите ми се издадоха, изпъкнаха, разшириха се;
        Зениците се опнаха до болка и тогава с набъбнало око
        об:схванах телата. –
Всичко е органично, това е моят Изток.
И опулен, оцъклен се изсмях.
И за първи път Историята и Географията имаха общ
Знаме:нател.
Те го – те:

v REVIEWING THE WAR

There it is.
When I looked back I saw the Black Sea was solid –
Corpses: so many millions, decomposing giant
                    bodies, I couldn't fit them in
                    the scope of my at:tension –
I strained – and my eyes widened, dilated, protruded;
          my pupils stretched painfully and with a swollen eye
          I per(re)ceived the bodies –
Everything is organic, this is my East.
And eyes wide, eyes glazed, I laughed out loud.
And for the first time History and Geography shared a common
Denominator.
Here it is:

W. N. HERBERT

AFTERWARDS

It seems that I've arrived here afterwards,
but Sofia, named for wisdom, doesn't say:
the world I've missed won't sit in any words.

It was the same in Moscow, Beijing – blurred
by jetlag, all the stars were rolled away
they told me, and I'd landed afterwards.

The statutes rip, the statues tip, the birds
return to sing upon dictators' graves –
the world's a mist that shifts, in other words.

So Palaeologos, lost in sickle swords,
threw Byzantium and his purple robe away –
then I arrived, long after afterwards.

And even in my own land, all the hoards
are long since ransacked and their skulls displayed,
the world I've missed won't sit in canny words.

So Sofia, swaddled in the empires' shrouds,
lets me discover her in disarray.
I know that I've arrived at afterwards,
and the world, once missed, won't fit just any words.

AN APPROACH

So much plaster has fallen from her walls
she feels like *lokum* or an unpeeled lychee
with its stalk still attached but not to a bush.
Down the side of an apartment block
in yellow visiting letters it says SOFCOM.

The light switches in the agency hostel are round
like discoloured eyeballs in black sockets.
Old gloss drips across the eyes of disenchanted
journalists. Flick them and they sound like big fat drops
on big fat roses; click, and the drops sound cold.

Lokum – a gelatinous confection, often flavoured with rose water and covered in
    powdered sugar.

The Largo's yellow bricks taste of a dust
that you suspect is worn-out turmeric.
The space where Zhivkov's tomb used to be
looks like the bristly disconnected jaw
of Desperate Dan, looks like a colossal chin.

Sitting on a stump with her black-clad back
to Vassil Levski Stadium, the art student sketches
a giant submachine gun upheld beyond
the closed booths and bare trees. The city smells
of rain as it is anticipated, rain as it falls.

GHOST GUESTS

The staff at the Bulgarian Telegraph Agency explain
our collaboration with the finest younger Bulgarian poets
must not disturb the ghosts of former journalists
who are still reporting events they can no longer attend,
that they never in fact attended,
who are typing up the news that never happened,
and quoting all the dignitaries
who still haven't spoken.

We must keep *shtum*: there are typewriters inside
those small dead skulls
still clacking dryly into the limestone
of keenly journalistic frontal lobes,
and the ghosts, who do not sleep above us,
must not be distracted – even by
our clicking Esperanto *na billiardski* – especially while
the staff attempt to watch Juventus.

The staff's large dogs either protect us
from wolves, mafia, and owl-shaped assassins,
or they prevent us from leaving.
Like the ghosts, thirsty for unbroken stories,
they sprawl around all day
while we, guests of a genus
unable to shower or buy *Zagorka* beer,
advance the dialogue of nations.

HRAM-PAMETNIK ALEKSANDER NEVSKI

*Hope allows us to deceive ourselves into thinking that life is parcelled
into discrete chunks – that our lives are stories with beginnings, middles
and ends.*

David Byrne, The New Sins

This whole cathedral feels inverted by
its brightly white-walled, icon-packed-out crypt;
that groaning well above more like a pit,
a funnel into earth instead of sky.

Post-Ottoman, it's only a reflection
of what these panels would have liked to found:
a nation's birth delivered through the wounds
that Georgi and Dimitar took with unction

and here inflict on dragon and on Turk
in mirrored blows, these warrior saints who poise
their name days at the seasons' gates, who pose
on rearing mounts against their dawns and darks

like scissors snipping out the fissive truth
that centuries can pass without a hope
while rebel songs meet silence on a rope –
this whole room's painted by those dying breaths.

It's in the miracle – that boy, unsure-
ly perched behind Georgi, somehow plucked
from the emir's side, still gripping at the jug
of Cretan water he was poised to pour.

It's in the ready martyrdoms – these rows
of butchered haloes who all trust their fears
will writhe upon Dimitar's needle spear –
he shakes his beard and it begins to snow.

And later at the launch for some new book
that claims to know our sins' new names, folk yelled
and drank wine like a hive of infidels,
till in the middle of that mell I looked

across to the cathedral through a square
of statues sinking into snow, as though
we'd drunk or cursed above into below,
and made earth cloud, and all these crystal prayers.

I went out, felt the chill and watched the flakes
ascend to line the statues' lids with grief
or paint flecks, those white letters that belief
forms from the gasps we force from dying necks.

DVOYANKA

Last night we ate from *Unter den Linden*,
the Restaurant of the Knowledge of Enlightenment Europe
and Bulgarian Cuisine, and in between
the scything of the *gadulka* and laconic taps on a *tupan*

I heard the double flute, that open-legged compass
of ancient, vase-based bacchanals – but chastened,
swung shut here, resembling a pencil case,
a long wood box emitting parallel melodies.

Later, we walked home past the vacant stone face
of a statue of former Socialist plenty,
clutching cold sheaves like corrected testaments;

and the *Sunshine Store*, selling stockings to a darkened street –
upended limbs spidered with tights,
legs splayed in a colder display.

Dvoyanka – the double flute

RED LULLABY

for Andy Croft

Hush little baby, don't feel worse,
Momma's going to buy you a talking horse,
a talking horse that wants to fly
and never tells a single lie.
The horse's mane is blow-torch white
to keep your crib aflame by night,
the horse's saddle strawberry red
to match the eyelids on your head,
the horse's hooves are made of steel
to keep your bedroom cold and real.
And if this truthful horse won't fly,
we'll bake its guts in humble pie;
and if this talking beast won't speak,
we'll dine on steak for half a week.

A DOUBLE BLESSING

The mind makes bad museums out of time
in which it stacks the icons of the eye:
one hand, out of the host of hands they raised
to bless me, all Sofia's swarm of saints;
one hand distracts because beneath it floats
the sketch of its first gesture like a ghost.

Those fingers reach out for a different chord –
some *mudra* that just might have, like a sword,
split church from church, was painted over here
but not quite painted out. As sailors read
dawn air for traces of familiar islands,
I read a clutch of memories in that hand.

As children on our first small trips abroad,
its suns broke up our northern clouds like bread
and spread out foreignness as something sweet;
our palates knew already, as they ate
their strange new words that tasted old as earth,
arrival was a paradox like birth.

Small voyages – across the gilt lagoon
to Venice, built on pillaged holy loot;
or Varna's Roman boatyards, drowned out by
a giant statue for a giant lie –
that workers wanted what the Party willed –
I saw and didn't see what these concealed.

Till Kerkira rewrote an islet as
a ship caught up by metamorphosis,
just as its rudder rooted into rock,
that visual echo grounded myth in shock
and made Ulysses' exile seem as real,
as tactile as his petrifying keel.

The adult tightens his pedantic grip
upon the senses' helm: for him that ship
is overwhelmed by ideology;
each trip asserts its iconology
from failings and the failure to feel blessed,
departure seems another little death.

As mast and sail were blown to conifers,
a crew made owls or mice at some god's curse,
so every sainted hand and golden chapel
saw Venice reascribe Constantinople,
and that colossal isolated girl
called wisdom by a Socialistic world.

So fingers under fingers point us back
to what we hold and what our holdings lack:
inside Cyrillic sits its kin's physique,
long-boned Byzantium, the way that Greek
still spills that infants' glimpse of alphabet,
those hot geometries that hold our breath.

And so this doubled hand is like a film,
two cells imposed within a single frame
that show a cog of history begin
to turn: the present's never just a brim
beneath which an unreaching grip extends,
it is the blessing that we cannot end.

ANDY CROFT was born in 1956. He moved to the North East in 1983 to teach in adult education. Writing-residencies include HMP Holme House and the Great North Run. Among his books are *Red Letter Days*, *Out of the Old Earth* (with Graeme Rigby), *A Weapon in the Struggle*, *Selected Poems of Randall Swingler*, *Comrade Heart*, *Holme and Away*, *Speaking English*, *Red Sky at Night* (with Adrian Mitchell), *North by North East* (with Cynthia Fuller) and thirty-seven books for teenagers, mostly about football. His books of poetry include *Nowhere Special*, *Gaps Between Hills* (with Dermot Blackburn and Mark Robinson), *Headland*, *Just as Blue*, *Great North*, *Comrade Laughter* and *The Ghost Writer*. He runs Smoke-stack Books and lives in Middlesbrough.

KRISTIN DIMITROVA was born in Sofia in 1963. She was educated at the University of Sofia, where she now teaches in the Department of Foreign Languages. Her books of poetry include *Jacob's Thirteenth Child* (1992), *A Face Under the Ice* (1997), *Closed Figures* (1998), *Faces with Twisted Tongues* (1998), *Talisman Repair* (2001) and *The People with the Lanterns* (2003). She has published a book of short-stories, *Love and Death under the Crooked Pear Tree* (2004). She has also translated a selection of poems by John Donne into Bulgarian. Her poems have been translated into Croatian, Dutch, German, Greek, Hungarian, Icelandic, French, Italian, Lithuanian, Macedonian, Persian, Polish, Russian, Serbian, Swedish and Turkish. A selection of her poems in English is published as *A Visit to the Clockmaker* (Southword Editions, Cork, 2005). From 2004-6, she was an editor of *Art Trud*, the weekly supplement for arts and culture of the largest Bulgarian daily newspaper. She lives in Sofia.

LINDA FRANCE was born in Newcastle upon Tyne. After some time living away, she moved back to the North East in 1981. She currently lives close to Hadrian's Wall in Northumberland. Her poetry collections, published by Bloodaxe Books, include *The Simultaneous Dress* (2002) and *The Toast of the Kit Cat Club* (2005), a biography in verse of the eighteenth-century traveller and writer Lady Mary Wortley Montagu. She also edited the acclaimed anthology *Sixty Women Poets* (Bloodaxe, 1993).

Linda France has worked on a number of collaborations with visual artists and musicians and over twenty Public Art projects. She currently teaches Creative Writing at the University of Newcastle.

GEORGI GOSPODINOV (b. 1968) is one of the most well known and translated younger Bulgarian writers. His first two books of poetry *Lapidarium* (1992) and *The Cherry-Tree of One People* (1996, reissued 1998 and 2003; Best Book Annual Award of the Association of Bulgarian Writers) were well received by readers and critics. His debut novel, *Natural Novel* (1999, 2000, 2004) was published in eight countries, including the USA, France, Denmark, the Czech REpublic and Serbia. Gospodinov's next book *And Other Stories* (2001), a collection of short stories, came out in France, the Czech Republic and Austria. His latest poetry collection is *Letters to Gaustin*. Georgi Gospodinov is editor of *Literaturen vestnik*, a literary and cultural weekly.

W. N. HERBERT was born in Dundee in 1961, and educated there and at Brasenose College, Oxford, where he published his D.Phil. thesis on the Scots poet Hugh MacDiarmid with OUP in 1992. In 2000 he edited the bestselling anthology *Strong Words: modern poets on modern poetry* with Matthew Hollis. He has published seven volumes of poetry and four pamphlets, and he is widely anthologised. His last five collections, all with the northern publisher Bloodaxe, have won numerous accolades. His most recent Bloodaxe collection, *Bad Shaman Blues*, appeared in March 2006 and is a PBS Recommendation. He is Professor of Poetry and Creative Writing at Newcastle University, and lives in an old lighthouse in North Shields with the novelist and editor Debbie Taylor, and their daughter Izzie.

NADYA RADULOVA (b. 1975) graduated from the Faculty of Slavic Studies, Sofia University in 1999. In 2001 she acquired her M.Phil. degree from Central European University, Budapest, and The Open University. Her academic interests are in the fields of Comparative Literature, Gender Studies, and literary translation.

Radulova also works as an editor of the monthly journal for gender, language and culture *altera*, and as a translator of poetry and fiction. She is the author of three books of poetry: *Tongue-tied Name* (1996), *Albas* (2000), and *Cotton, Glass and Electricity* (2004). Her works have been translated into English, Russian, Czech, and Turkish.

MARK ROBINSON was born in Preston, Lancashire in 1964 and now lives in the parish of Preston-on-Tees in Eaglescliffe. His poetry collections include *Half a Mind, Gaps Between Hills* (with Andy Croft and Dermot Blackburn), *The Horse Burning Park* and *The Domesticity Remix*. His work has been widely anthologised and translated.

He edited *Write Out Loud*, a ground-breaking collection of essays on poetry readings. For ten years, he edited *Scratch* poetry magazine and press. In 2000, a film featuring one of his poems won a Regional Television Society award.

He enjoys a parallel life as Executive Director of Arts Council England, North East.

VBV (b. 1977) writes both poetry and prose and has published three books: *Th:is* (2000), *From Th:is* (2002), and *Typographische Raume: Typographic Rooms* (2004). He has won several awards for his prose and poetry.

He is a sponsor and Editor-in-Chief of *Red.groo* (1998), a virtual editors group which publishes manifestos every two years.

Other anthologies of poetry in translation
published by Arc Publications
include:

Altered State: An Anthology of New Polish Poetry
EDS. ROD MENGHAM, TADEUSZ PIÓRO, PIOTR SZYMOR
Translated by Rod Mengham, Tadeusz Pióro *et al*

A Fine Line: New Poetry from Eastern
& Central Europe
EDS. JEAN BOASE-BEIER, ALEXANDRA BÜCHLER, FIONA SAMPSON
Various translators

6 Slovenian Poets
ED. BRANE MOZETIČ
Translated by Ana Jelnikar, Kelly Lenox Allen
and Stephen Watts
with an introduction by Aleš Debalek

6 Basque Poets
ED. MARI JOSE OLAZIREGI
Translated by Amaia Gabantxo

The Page and The Fire:
Russian Poets on Russian Poets
ED. PETER ORAM
Translated and introduced by
Peter Oram